HOW CONFUCIUS
CHANGED MY MIND

HOW CONFUCIUS CHANGED MY MIND

And What He Can Teach You about the Art of Being Human

CHARLES B. JONES

SHAMBHALA

Shambhala Publications, Inc.
2129 13th Street
Boulder, Colorado 80302
www.shambhala.com

The Analects excerpts are sourced from James Legge's *The Chinese Classics: With
Translation, Critical and Exegetical Notes, Prolegomena, and Copious Indexes*,
vol. 1 (London: Trübner, 1861), retrieved online via the Chinese Text Project,
https://ctext.org/analects.
The *Doctrine of the Mean* excerpts are sourced from James Legge's *Sacred Books
of the East*, vol. 28, part 4: "The Li Ki" (Oxford: Clarendon Press, 1885), retrieved
online via the Chinese Text Project, https://ctext.org/liji/zhong-yong.

Cover art: © Vanni Archive / Art Resource, NY

9 8 7 6 5 4 3 2 1

First Edition
Printed in the United States of America

Shambhala Publications makes every effort to print on acid-free, recycled paper.
Shambhala Publications is distributed worldwide by Penguin Random House,
Inc., and its subsidiaries.

Library of Congress Cataloging-in-Publication Data
Names: Jones, Charles Brewer, 1957– author.
Title: How Confucius changed my mind: and what he can teach you about the
art of being human/Charles B. Jones.
Description: First edition. | Boulder, Colorado: Shambhala, [2025] |
Includes bibliographical references and index.
Identifiers: LCCN 2024028234 | ISBN 9781645472995 (trade paperback)
Subjects: LCSH: Philosophy, Confucian. | Confucianism. | East Asia—Religion.
Classification: LCC B127.65 J56 2025 | DDC 181/.112—dc23/eng/20241101
LC record available at https://lccn.loc.gov/2024028234

The authorized representative in the EU for product safety and
compliance is eucomply OÜ, Pärnu mnt 139b-14, 11317 Tallinn, Estonia,
hello@eucompliancepartner.com.

CONTENTS

Preface   vii

Note on Orthography   xi

Note on Sources   xii

1. Confucius, Mencius, Xunzi, and Me   1
2. Ritual Propriety, Appropriateness, and the Confucian Self   15
3. The Way (*Dao*)   39
4. The Princely Man, the Sage, Sincerity, and Humanity   55
5. Human Nature   79
6. Personal Cultivation   97
7. Dissenters   121
8. How Did Confucius Change My Mind?   137

For Further Reading   147

Notes   149

Works Cited   155

Index   157

About the Author   162

PREFACE

About ten years into my college teaching career, I decided to start wearing a coat and tie to class. Prior to that, I was likely to wear jeans (blue or black) and a shirt with the sleeves rolled up, and maybe a sweater if the weather was cold. I thought of my classroom as an egalitarian space where the students and I gathered to explore ideas together. I encouraged free discussion based on the day's readings and tried to make sure all voices were heard without always privileging my own.

This all seemed very nice according to my upbringing in Western—specifically, North American—culture, but I knew all along that it was not working as well as I wanted. Students would tell me that they weren't ready for open discussion because the ideas I was teaching and the texts they were reading were too foreign. They needed me to explain things to them through lectures. The posture of role equality also proved difficult to sustain. After all, they knew I was not going to go out to the bars with them on a Friday night, and more seriously, I still had the responsibility of grading their work. We were not peers in reality and to pretend that we were felt inauthentic and misleading.

I found the help I needed in my reading and teaching of East Asian religions, including my course on Daoism and Confucianism. I knew that Confucian thought presumes that human beings in society live in hierarchies where almost all relationships are between individuals on different levels (the sole exception being that between friends). I also had learned that behavior within these hierarchies was governed by ritual actions that set boundaries and established expectations and obligations between people of unequal rank. Like many Westerners, I found these strictures artificial and antidemocratic at first, and I much preferred the naturalness and spontaneity of the Daoist texts and masters.

In time, however, I came to appreciate the value of Confucian thought. I could not deny that my students and I were not meeting as peers, and it became increasingly clear that the college class was a ritual situation, whether we acknowledged it or not. I decided to try the Confucian way: I put on a coat and tie to ritually mark the difference in status and adopted a somewhat more formal manner. The students naturally fell into calling me "Dr. Jones" as I continued to address them by their first names. To my surprise, relations between my students and me improved. I had been afraid that this new arrangement would make class stiff and inhibiting, but instead I found that our relationships became warmer and more relaxed. It turned out that clear boundaries and role expectations signaled by conventional symbols and behaviors made things much easier for everyone. Hierarchy did not exclude mutuality.

That is what this book is about. It is not a textbook on Confucian history and thought but a record of the surprising ways in which the encounter with this tradition changed me and my students. Describing these changes will, of course, require that we spend some time understanding Confucius and his followers, but the final goal is to show you the benefits of deep engagement with other systems of thought or culture.

This book is also not an attempt to show that Confucianism is "relevant" to you, nor does it seek to recommend that anyone adopt Confucianism as their religion or practice in toto. There are many aspects of Confucianism that would likely not work very well in Western settings, and a wholesale adoption of Confucianism by individuals or groups outside East Asia would engender new problems.

So, what are we doing, then? Two things primarily:

1. I want to model a fruitful way of engaging with a very foreign way of thinking that avoids two problematic approaches. The first is the tendency to think that, as human beings, we ought to be able to understand one another quite easily in a short time. This book will show that understanding others takes work and patience. If we jump too quickly to conclusions, we are likely to project our own beliefs and behaviors onto the other. Real understanding requires we become aware of things we believe on such a deep level that we do not even know we believe them. This helps us avoid superimposing these beliefs uncritically on others. Without knowing how deep the differences actually go, it is all too easy to look at others and just see ourselves reflected back.

The second tendency is to view cultural and linguistic groups as utterly separate from one another and to believe that no real understanding is possible. In this view, only the "insiders" know their own cultures and customs, while "outsiders" will never really get it. This book contends that intercultural understanding is not a binary you-either-get-it-or-you-don't proposition but a continual effort that yields improvements over time. Even if we never attain insider's knowledge, we can still approximate it more closely the longer we apply ourselves to the task. The payoff is an expansion of our conceptual frameworks. The best comment I ever received at the end of one of my courses was "I didn't know it was even possible to think like that."

2. Engagement with another tradition can lead us to see our own traditions with fresh eyes. Our culture encompasses many beliefs and practices, but a dominant rhetoric can cause us to see some of them better than others. The value we place on creativity, originality, individualism, and nonconformity hides from our

view just how much our behavior is ritualized and how much has been handed down to us. When my classroom embraced its inherent ritual nature, I found that we did not have to invent anything from scratch. The rituals and roles already existed in Western educational culture, and once I gave the cue by my change of attire and manner, the students already knew what to do. This points to another finding from my study of Confucianism: As foreign as it might seem, much of it is already present in our culture. We do not always see it because our discourses of individualism and egalitarianism keep us from noticing.

I hope that this book will encourage and enable you to share the journey I have been on over the last thirty years of teaching. The rewards are great and well worth the trip.

NOTE ON ORTHOGRAPHY

This book will use the pinyin system for rendering Chinese words and names. This is an internationally accepted system that reflects the pronunciation of words in Mandarin, the *putonghua*, or "common speech," of modern China. It will except names that are already well known in other spellings, notably Confucius and Mencius as well as other names that are better known under alternative romanizations (e.g., Wing-tsit Chan rather than Chen Rongjie). A few of these spellings are not entirely clear to people not familiar with Chinese pronunciation, so the following should help with some of the more difficult letters.

C: a hard, aspirated "ts," as in *cats*

X: a kind of "sh" sound, but with the tip of the tongue touching the back of the bottom front teeth, producing a bit of a hiss

Zh: a very hard "j" sound made with the tongue curled upward so the tip points to the roof of the mouth

Q: a kind of "ch" sound, with the tongue positioned as described above for *X*

Ü: pronounced the same as a "u" with an umlaut in German or French (note that after j, q, and x, "u" is also pronounced this way even though no umlaut is used)

Z: Pronounced "dz," like the "ds" in *kids*

NOTE ON SOURCES

The citations from the *Analects* of Confucius follow the book and verse numbering found in James Legge's translation. See "Works Cited" for details. In these citations I have substituted my preferred translations for certain key terms to maintain consistency. I have indicated these changes by putting the term in square brackets. For example, "gentleman" becomes "[princely man]."

A few citations from neo-Confucian authors come from Wing-tsit Chan's *Source Book in Chinese Philosophy*. See "Works Cited" for details.

In all citations, I have changed older spellings to modern pinyin.

The translations from the books of *Mencius*, *Xunzi*, and *Mozi* are mine.

HOW CONFUCIUS
CHANGED MY MIND

1

CONFUCIUS, MENCIUS, XUNZI, AND ME

This book deals primarily with an encounter, so we will begin by introducing the main characters. We will briefly examine the lives of Confucius and his two most prominent heirs, Mencius and Xunzi, and finish with an account of myself as an early-career teacher trying to find a way to make Confucianism interesting to Western students.

孔子
CONFUCIUS (C. 551–C. 479 B.C.E.)

Analects 7.1
The Master said, "A transmitter and not a maker, believing in and loving the ancients, I venture to compare myself with our old Peng."[1]

Analects 7.2
The Master said, "The silent treasuring up of knowledge; learning without satiety; and instructing others without being wearied—which one of these things belongs to me?"

Analects 7.3

The Master said, "The learning virtue without proper cultivation; the not thoroughly discussing what is learned; not being able to move towards righteousness of which a knowledge is gained; and not being able to change what is not good—these are the things which occasion me solicitude."

Analects 7.4

When the Master was unoccupied with business, his manner was easy, and he looked pleased.

Analects 7.7

The Master said, "From the man bringing his bundle of dried flesh for my teaching upwards, I have never refused instruction to anyone."

Analects 7.9

When the Master was eating by the side of a mourner, he never ate to the full.

Analects 7.14

When the Master was in Qi, he heard the Shao, and for three months did not know the taste of flesh. He said, "I did not think that music could have been made so excellent as this."

Analects 7.38

The Master was mild, and yet dignified; majestic, and yet not fierce; respectful, and yet easy.

Confucius saw everything falling apart in an empire that had once been great. According to history as he understood it, the Zhou dynasty had mounted a rebellion against the previous Shang dynasty five hundred years before his birth. They owed the success of their revolt to the depravity of the last Shang emperors and the exemplary virtue of the first Zhou kings. The moral differential had led Heaven (*tian*) to withdraw its mandate (*ming*) from the Shang and transfer it to the Zhou. By Confucius's time, the concept of Heaven had evolved from a celestial divinity to a more impersonal natural force. Nevertheless, this force took note of human moral conduct, especially within the ruling house, and would lend its support to those who acted for the good of the people.

The problem in Confucius's time was that the Zhou ruling house had become weak and its various vassal states had broken away, becoming independent in all but name. Warfare raged constantly, local ruling dynasties came and went in quick succession, civil wars broke out within them, treachery was rampant, and the common people suffered under rulers who cared only for their own self-aggrandizement. Surely this was causing Heaven to take its mandate away from the Zhou dynasty, and the result could only be further turmoil, natural disasters, and foreign invasion. Something had to be done to rectify the situation.

Many thinkers came forward over the following decades to propose solutions. Mozi said that people needed to know that a just God was watching them, ready to punish wrongdoing. The Legalists proposed that a strong central government implement a policy of law and order with strict enforcement. Daoist thinkers either recommended a government that flowed with the circumstances or a retreat away from politics into nature. (See chapter 7 for more information on these dissents.) Confucius looked to restore a past golden age when the early Zhou rulers governed with virtue and earned Heaven's Mandate. If he could convince present rulers to rectify their conduct and rule their people with benevolence, then Heaven would renew its mandate and the land would return to peace and prosperity. The key lay in discovering what the early Zhou rulers did in as much detail as possible, so Confucius went about collecting as many archival texts as he could in order to reconstruct their practices. What he found was an attention to ritual performance that helped to cement the ruler's relationship with the moral force that connected nature to human relations. This may surprise modern readers who believe that pragmatic measures would be more likely to produce the desired outcome, but given Confucius's background, perhaps this is not such an odd proposition after all.

Confucius came from the state of Lu on the northeastern coast of modern China. His family, surnamed Kong, had migrated there a few generations earlier from the state of Song just to the south. They had been minor aristocrats and were possibly descended from the Shang ruling house. Song was where the early Zhou rulers had resettled some of the upper-class families of the conquered dynasty in order that they might continue the rites associated with the Shang. These families maintained the belief that the Shang, though militarily weaker than the Zhou, had been culturally more advanced: they had music, writing, and the arts, things in which the Zhou lagged behind or lacked altogether. Over the centuries, the people of Song had continued to wear distinctive clothing and use speech patterns that had gradually become antiquated.

At the same time, the turmoil of the times had led to the appearance of a class of men called *ru*. The *ru* came from aristocratic families throughout the empire. Sometimes the families were dispossessed or down on their luck; sometimes they were so successful that they had produced too many male heirs to give all of them land and titles. Some had been conquered by other families and had escaped. Whatever the case, they were men of education and manners who would not simply assimilate into the mass of commoners. With their skills, education, and experience, they presented themselves at the castles and mansions of other powerful families to offer their services. They might tutor the young sons of the household, or they might take up military commands, serve as scribes and archivists to write and file official documents, or advise rulers on policy matters, court protocols, and rituals. There were many such men seeking positions in Confucius's day.

This meant that the boy named Kong Qiu or Kong Zhongni had two different heritages upon which to draw. As a *ru*, he had the abilities necessary to seek government employment. As a native of Lu and possibly a descendant of the Shang ruling house, he stood apart from other *ru* because of his distinctive dress and manners. However, these two factors are not sufficient to explain his eminence within Chinese civilization. The decisive factor was his determination to make a difference. He would not be content merely to do the bidding of any ruler if it meant adding to the troubles of the time. He sought a position as a court adviser high enough to be able to suggest policies and practices that would advance his vision of renewing the Way of the Ancient Kings.

This would not be easy for a young man who had lost his father early in life and had educated himself. Without the connections that well-placed relatives or teachers could provide, he had to push himself forward through his own talent and diligence. For a time, he held minor posts as an administrator of pastures and superintendent of grains for a powerful local family in Lu, but he wanted more. He began to take in students who did not come from elite backgrounds, and for this he is honored as the first private teacher to this day. He himself was so fond of teaching and learning that he said he would gladly take in any student, even one who only had some dried meat to offer for tuition, provided the student had the diligence and aptitude to learn. Thus, for his students, he represented a possible path of upward social mobility, as through his teaching they could gain the skills needed for high government posts.

They were right. At least nine of his students eventually gained prestigious appointments on the strength of the humanistic education and specific skills he had given them. Through them, Confucius eventually attained official employment, but not of the kind he desired. Some rulers felt it was unseemly for students to have official positions when their teacher did not, but they also did not want to listen to his ideas or endure his corrections. In the end, he found his posts were largely ceremonial and did not give him the opportunity to advise rulers on policy questions.

He did not give up on his dream of making a difference in the world, however. Late in his life, he took to the road, stopping at various courts to seek employment. For thirteen years he went from one place to another, often staying for extended periods of time and receiving stipends, often being driven out or escaping from danger. Nowhere did he get the kind of job he craved, perhaps because his message to rulers was not to their liking: rulers were to govern by virtue; the measure of their success was the happiness of their subjects, not the extent to which they filled their own coffers; proper attention to ritual was the key to gaining and keeping the Mandate of Heaven, and so on. On one occasion his criticism of those in power even led to an assassination attempt. After years of disappointment, he returned home to Lu at the age of sixty-eight.

While he may have judged his long journey a failure, in fact it is most likely the reason he is remembered to this day. It enabled him to spread his message across the entire northern and northeastern tiers of states, and while on the road he amassed a cache of archival texts that he would spend his remaining days editing into works that became the classics of the tradition. He continued to take in students, and he is still credited with establishing the institution of private schools offering education to anyone of ability from any background. September 10 is still celebrated as

"Teacher's Day" in Confucius temples all around China and the Chinese diaspora.

Confucius died at the age of seventy-three at home surrounded by friends and students. With his death his teaching passed into various lineages of masters and disciples, where his ideas were developed and elaborated. Two of the most significant bearers of his tradition in the centuries following his death were Mencius and Xunzi.

Before leaving Confucius, though, I want to call attention to the quotations at the beginning of this section that depict his character and deportment, for in the sources these observations count just as much as what he taught for commending the Sage to us as worthy of our attention. In these descriptions we see a man who, while specializing in ritual matters, remained aware that the purpose of ritual was not to oppress people into inauthentic behaviors but to help them relate to one another better. Thus, we do not find him to be overly scrupulous about his own behavior or too much of a martinet in correcting others. He remains affable, grounded, and generous; he refrains from indulging himself out of consideration for the feelings of a friend in grief; and he can be polite and reserved while remaining friendly. As we will see later, the purpose of study in ancient Chinese thought is not to accumulate a body of facts but to refine one's character, and so it is these testimonials to the way Confucius moved through the world that made him worthy of attention and emulation. His students wanted to listen to his lessons so that they could be more like him.

His influence on Chinese culture cannot be overestimated. In the late sixteenth century, Jesuit missionaries saw this and, needing to report back to the church and their superiors in Europe on the state of the field, had to render his name into Latin. For the Chinese, Confucius is just "Kongzi," or "Master Kong," as seen in the Chinese characters at the head of this section. Wishing to stress his eminence even over other thinkers in the tradition, they inserted the character *fu* into his name to designate him as a "great master," and afterward they latinized "Kongfuzi" into "Confucius," the name by which those outside China know him to the present day.

孟子
MENCIUS (372–289 B.C.E.)

Like "Confucius," "Mencius" is a latinized form of the name Mengzi, or "Master Meng." He was a fourth-generation student of Confucius, having studied under the latter's grandson Zisi. Even before Mencius was born, conditions in northern China had changed in ways that pushed thinkers of all schools to deepen and systematize their teachings.

Not long after Confucius's death, China entered the Warring States period (475–221 B.C.E.), which lasted until the Qin dynasty conquered all its rivals in 221 B.C.E. Confucius lived during a previous era called the Spring and Autumn period, named after the work that chronicled its history, the *Spring and Autumn Annals*. This refers to the chaos that ensued after a major uprising against the Zhou dynasty in the eighth century B.C.E., which led to the political breakdown with which people were still coping during Confucius's day. During this time, petty states and warlords arose and fell in quick succession, which was why the *ru* were able to find positions as tutors and court functionaries so readily; there were a lot of small courts that needed organizing and a lot of new rulers who needed help making the transition from field general to statesman.

The Warring States period was different. By this time, a few ruling houses had been very successful in conquering neighbors and consolidating their rule over larger territories. This meant fewer courts and more competition: the itinerant teachers and courtiers who sought work had to compete more directly for appointments. Aspirants to court positions might need to demonstrate their superiority to others on the scene. With more applicants vying for fewer positions, everyone had to improve his abilities in debate in order to take on the competition.

More significantly, the northern state of Qi set up what may be the world's first think tank in their capital city in 318 B.C.E. The Jixia Academy ("the Academy below the Ji gate") put out a call for the best and the brightest from around the subcontinent, and all who were accepted received housing and a stipend. All they had to do in return was develop their ideas and debate them publicly. The ruling house's motivations for establishing this academy are unclear, but it had a lasting impact on the development of early Chinese thought. Confucius had never had to debate his ideas in an abstract way; his only mission was to equip his students with the knowledge and temperament they would need for official employment. Now, however, thinkers from all over put their ideas into direct confrontation, leading to their refinement and systematization. Mencius was at the academy at its founding and remained in residence for a few years. Xunzi seems to have been its dean for ten years.

As to Mencius's biography, little is known about him. His father died young, and legend has it that his mother went to extraordinary lengths to ensure his education. After his studies, he spent most of his life in imitation of Confucius, going from one court to another looking for a post and frequently failing. Like Confucius, he taught that the purpose of government was not the enrichment of the ruling house but the happiness and prosperity of the people. Once, a ruler asked Mencius how to gain more profit, but Mencius deflected the question and admonished the ruler that righteousness was far more important. His dictum that the people had a right to rebel against a tyrant was even less welcome.

While Mencius did offer much by way of practical advice—as when he counseled against starting a military campaign during the harvest season when men needed to be in the fields—the teaching that will concern us most in this book will be that human nature is wholly good. Confucius had not pronounced on this issue, but the intellectual atmosphere of Mencius's day required him to address it. We will see that "human nature" means something very different in Confucian thought than it does in Western philosophy, and coming to understand its meaning in context will help us to explore what Confucian thinkers thought it meant to be human.

荀子
XUNZI (C. 310–AFTER 238 B.C.E.)

Xunzi, or Master Xun, was a near-contemporary of Mencius, but it is unlikely the two ever met. (I once knew a professor from China with the same surname, and her advice for helping Westerners pronounce "Xun" was to think of Schwinn bicycles.) Very little is known of his life outside the fact that he studied at and was later the dean at the Jixia Academy, meaning that he knew the major currents of thought of his day and critiqued them all. According to some sources, he was so unpleasant to his philosophical rivals that he was eventually run out of the academy and journeyed south to the state of Chu. After that the trail goes cold. However, the fact that he spent so much of his adult life in an institute of higher learning means that his writings are exceptionally well preserved, so we can know what he thought in great detail.

We know him primarily as taking a view on human nature diametrically opposed to that of Mencius. While Mencius believed human nature was wholly good, Xunzi believed it was completely evil. However, as we shall see in chapter 5, the two are not as opposed to each other as this seems to indicate. Rather, they used different definitions and reasons for their conclusions, and in the end, they are not very far apart. Another idea that we will examine later is that ritual is not just for organizing and smoothing human activities and relations. Xunzi believed we need ritual because it is inherently beautiful, and human beings need beauty.

. . . AND ME

As noted at the beginning of this chapter, this is not just another textbook on Confucianism. While I do hope that by the end you will have gained enough of a foundation in Confucian ways of thinking to pursue further study on your own, I am writing primarily about my encounter with this tradition and the ways in which it shifted my outlook. Put another way, I want you to be *motivated* to read further by bearing witness to the benefits I have gained through my engagement with Confucianism.

If I am to describe a "shift" in my own thinking, I need to say a bit about where I was prior to my encounter with the tradition.

I entered my doctoral program at the University of Virginia in January 1989 to study East Asian Buddhism. Like many, I was fascinated by its teachings, which pointed beyond everyday affairs, and its goals of enlightenment and liberation. However, professors do not always get to follow their primary passions, and when I began teaching in the early 1990s, I was assigned courses such as World Religions and Religions of Asia. This required me to gain a working knowledge of other traditions, many of which, like Daoism, I found equally interesting. Confucianism, on the other hand, had a bad rap. Americans at the time regarded Confucius as a dispenser of fortune-cookie-grade maxims, and the comedian Redd Foxx had a whole series of "Confucius say . . ." jokes that reduced the philosopher's thought to a string of punch lines. Confucius seemed stuck in the mundane world of daily life, work, family, and government. His philosophy had much to say about how emperors should rule and how children should behave toward their parents, but nothing about the supernatural, mystical experience, life after death, enlightenment, or liberation. It spoke of ritual seemingly for ritual's sake, and I was left wondering how I was going to make this tradition interesting for my students when I was having a hard time mustering enthusiasm for it myself.

A slim seventy-five-page book helped me begin to appreciate Confucius. This was the philosopher Herbert Fingarette's *Confucius: The Secular as Sacred.* Prior to that book's appearance in 1972, the study of Confucius had been the province of historians and sinologists. Fingarette brought his expertise in philosophy to the *Analects* of Confucius and teased out underlying conceptual frames and linguistic subtleties that opened up Confucius the thinker for a Western audience. Following that, a series of books by the team of David Hall (a Western-trained philosopher) and Roger T. Ames (a specialist in Chinese intellectual history) extended the path Fingarette had opened and brought into clearer focus the distinctions between early Chinese and Western thought. It became apparent that understanding Confucianism (or any Asian system) required students to identify and bracket out cultural presuppositions that either led them to *think* they could understand Confucius easily (a problem made worse by having to read him in English translation) or stymied comprehension altogether.

At the same time, making the subject interesting meant I had to formulate concrete examples so that my students would understand what Confucius was saying. I created characters and stories to help students think through the issues for themselves and culled examples from real life to show that the situations Confucius discussed and critiqued were realistic. In many cases, I developed these stories and examples to answer questions students had raised. This led to a paradoxical realization: (1) Asian ways of thinking are quite different from Western ways, and communicating them to Western students requires a good deal of interpretation; while (2) in many cases, Confucius's analysis of human sociality held surprising relevance for understanding Western society by revealing aspects of our organization and behavior that our own cultural values prevented us from seeing. It is these insights and observations that inspired me to write this book.

Finally, as I have gotten older, I have found it both useful and comforting to delve into the legacy of a tradition that focused its attention on how we can make the best of ordinary life in this world. I even changed some of my own teaching practices and personal habits in light of the lessons I learned from it. Transcendence and enlightenment are still intriguing topics to be sure, but a thinker who spent his time pondering how we can maximize our humanity in the simple process of living with one another has something to tell us as well. In the following pages, we will grapple with how best to understand Confucius and his followers, and we will meet the characters whose foibles animate the stories I have used for a few decades to teach students to appreciate the insights of a thinker and reformer who lived twenty-five hundred years ago on the other side of the world.

2

RITUAL PROPRIETY, APPROPRIATENESS, AND THE CONFUCIAN SELF

This chapter will launch our journey by exploring the aspect of Confucianism that many find most tedious: the teaching of ritual propriety. Through an examination of his ideas about the proper performance of ritual infused with a quality called "appropriateness," you will discover that Confucius regarded this practice as the way we maximize our humanity. You will also find that even your own daily interactions are infused with ritual for many of the reasons Confucius offers. Later in the chapter we will see the surprising ways in which Confucius's recommendations about social rituals informed and were informed by his views on what it means to be human.

禮

RITUAL AND RITUAL PROPRIETY (*LI*)

Analects 1.12

The philosopher You said, "In practicing the rules of propriety, [harmony] is to be prized. In the ways prescribed by the ancient kings, this is the excellent quality, and in things small and great we follow them. Yet it is not to be observed in all cases. If one, knowing how such ease should be prized, manifests it, without regulating it by the rules of propriety, this likewise is not to be done."

In a society that values spontaneity and free self-expression, the teaching that human fulfillment begins with mastering ritual forms seems especially foreign. Even in Confucius's own time, there were rival thinkers such as the Daoist sage Zhuangzi who considered a life spent in ritual performance inauthentic (see chapter 7). We can understand Confucius's emphasis on ritual and ritual propriety a little better if we remember that his students were young men who aspired to government service and that life in a ruling court was thoroughly bound by ritual. Throughout imperial Chinese history, ministers appeared in court early in order to finish the day's business before the sun rose. They had to dress in the garb appropriate to their rank and role. They had to speak in formal terms that could vary according to their status relative to the status of the person being addressed. They had to be in their assigned place and assume the proper stance. More than that, the emperor himself presided over many rituals both great and small, and needed masters who could supervise their proper performance. Life was anything but spontaneous and expression was anything but free.

But Confucius saw more in ritual training than just the mastery of skills that qualified one to work for the emperor. Ritual mastery was the beginning point for proper human relationships and led to the right ordering of society, smooth relationships between people, and (*contra* Zhuangzi) the fulfillment of one's humanity. We will begin in this section with ritual itself and explore the idea of "appropriateness" (*yi*) in the next section.

Herbert Fingarette helpfully opened his discussion of ritual propriety by looking at a common social ritual: the handshake.[1] As a warm-up to this topic, I ask my students to think ahead to a day when they might have young children that they are trying to socialize. How would they teach a child the right way to shake hands? Which hand do you extend? The right hand. How firmly do you grasp the other person's hand? Firmly but not uncomfortably so, somewhere between the cold fish and the vise. How many times do you move your hands up and down? Two, maybe three times, but no more. What about eye contact? Yes, maintain eye contact. What might you say, assuming you are being introduced to someone for the first time? Some accepted phrases include "I'm pleased to meet you" or "How are you?" Later they can refine and vary the gesture, such as by learning to judge when it is appropriate to put the left hand on the other's shoulder, when to be more reserved, and so on.

We can think of ritual propriety, then, as the "how" of ritual, the procedures that we can describe and teach to others. It is useful because it gives us ways of interacting with people before we have established relationships with them, a point we can illustrate simply by asking what we might do if we did not have this social ritual. In such a situation, both we and the other person would be forced to improvise a way of indicating the desire to get a new relationship off on the right foot with no guarantee that it would go well. Ritual, then, functions as a kind of language that allows us to communicate social signals to others in a consistent and predictable way.

Once we become accustomed to looking at behaviors such as shaking hands as ritual, then it is not difficult to find rituals in other places as well. This is obvious in settings such as religious services, but it also shows up in more secular settings. An example that comes readily to mind is a teacher teaching a class. Just as with the handshake, it is possible to describe to a newcomer or a small child the etiquette of a traditional college classroom:

Students arrive on time. The teacher stands in front to deliver the lesson. Students address the teacher respectfully (in my classroom, I am "Dr. Jones" or "Professor"). Students should not have side conversations. Students signal their desire to ask a question by raising a hand and speaking after the teacher acknowledges them. The benefit to everyone is that the class runs smoothly, and no one has to wonder what they should do.

However, the example of the classroom raises a new issue. While a handshake may function regardless of the roles or status of the people involved, the ritual of the classroom prescribes different behaviors for the teacher and the students. This brings us to an important point about Confucianism: it presumes hierarchy and assigns different roles to people depending upon where they fit within it. Confucian texts frequently refer to the "five relationships": ruler to minister, father to son, husband to wife, elder brother to younger brother, and friend to friend. Of these five, only the last obtains between peers. The other four presume that the first member of the pair occupies a position of authority over the second. This seems to rub against the egalitarian impulses of modern Western culture.

Or does it? As I began my teaching career, I aspired to run my classes as cooperative learning communities free of status distinctions. It never worked very well, and I think it is because the students instantly saw through this pose. We were not friends or peers. I was not going to socialize with them on the weekends, and they knew I would be grading their work. After a few years, I understood what Confucius meant and I changed my approach. I began to wear a coat and tie to class, indicating by my dress that I did not occupy the same place in the classroom setting as my students. I became a bit more formal. In sum, I embraced my role as the teacher in this setting and treated my students as students. To my surprise, the atmosphere in my classroom improved. Clear boundaries and role expectations turned out to be the thing my students needed from me.

At the same time, I came to understand that the rituals associated with a given hierarchy did not apply in a meaningful way outside the boundaries within which that hierarchy mattered. For example, I do not insist that anyone outside of an academic setting address me as "Doctor" or "Professor." "Mr. Jones" will do nicely in other situations. The Confucian tradition does not place us in a single set of hierarchical relationships but makes room for the multiple and often overlapping structures within which we find ourselves. The challenge lies in managing these various social contexts without losing our feel for the proper rituals they each entail.

Thus, understanding Confucius's teaching about ritual propriety alerted me to look beyond my accustomed cultural discourse of spontaneity and equality. I could see that ritual (understood broadly to include what may seem to us mere "protocol") pervades our life together and provides a valuable service in enabling us to signal intentions and desires even to strangers, establish relationships smoothly, and work together productively. Like language, ritual provides a medium for communication and lends some regularity and consistency to our day-to-day interactions.

But having common ritual forms by itself is not enough.

APPROPRIATENESS (*YI*)

Analects 2.7

Zi You asked what filial piety was. The Master said, "The filial piety nowadays means the support of one's parents. But dogs and horses likewise are able to do something in the way of support; without reverence, what is there to distinguish the one support given from the other?"

Analects 3.4

Lin Fang asked what was the first thing to be attended to in [ritual]. The Master said, "A great question indeed! In festive [rituals], it is better to be sparing than extravagant. In the [rituals] of mourning, it is better that there be deep sorrow than a minute attention to observances."

Analects 3.26

The Master said, "High station filled without indulgent generosity; [rituals] performed without reverence; mourning conducted without sorrow—wherewith should I contemplate such ways?"

Analects 4.13

The Master said, "If a prince is able to govern his kingdom with the complaisance proper to [ritual] propriety, what difficulty will he have? If he cannot govern it with that complaisance, what has he to do with [ritual] propriety?"

Analects 9.3

The Master said, "The linen cap is that prescribed by [ritual propriety], but now a silk one is worn. It is economical, and I follow the common practice. Bowing below the hall is prescribed by [ritual propriety], but now the practice is to bow only after ascending it. That is arrogant. I continue to bow below the hall, though I oppose the common practice."

Analects 17.21

Zai Wo asked about the three years' mourning for parents, saying that one year was long enough. "If the [princely man] abstains for three years from the observances of [ritual] propriety, those observances will be quite lost. If for three years he abstains from music, music will be ruined. Within a year the old grain is exhausted, and the new grain has sprung up, and, in procuring fire by friction, we go through all the changes of wood for that purpose. After a complete year, the mourning may stop." The Master said, "If you were, after a year, to eat good rice, and wear embroidered clothes, would you feel at ease?" "I should," replied Wo. The Master said, "If you can feel at ease, do it. But a [princely man], during the whole period of mourning, does not enjoy pleasant food which he may eat, nor derive pleasure from music which he may hear. He also does not feel at ease, if he is comfortably lodged. Therefore he does not do what you propose. But now you feel at ease and may do it." Zai Wo then went out, and the Master said, "This shows Yu's want of virtue. It is not till a child is three years old that it is allowed to leave the arms of its parents. And the three years' mourning is universally observed throughout the empire. Did Yu enjoy the three years' love of his parents?"

Mencius 4A.17
Chunyu Kun said, "Is it in accordance with ritual propriety that men and women should not touch when giving and receiving things?" Mencius said, "It is the rite." [Chunyu Kun then] said, "If a man's sister-in-law is drowning, can he use his hand to rescue her then?" "[Mencius] said, "One who would not rescue his drowning sister-in-law is a wolf! That men and women should not touch is ritual propriety; to rescue one's drowning sister-in-law is a necessary contingency."

David Hall and Roger T. Ames point out that there is another word that comes up in the *Analects* that in most Confucian texts means "righteousness," but in this text they translate it as "appropriateness" (*yi*). To see what this is about, let me go back to the example of a handshake and describe a demonstration that I do in class. I approach two students and offer both a handshake done exactly as described above: I reach out with my right hand, make eye contact, use a suitably firm grasp, shake their hand two or three times, and say, "I'm pleased to meet you." Nevertheless, even though the two performances are identical in form and we may say I did them "correctly," there is one crucial difference. In the first instance, I appear interested and engaged, and my tone of voice is friendly and inviting. In the second, I affect a slightly bored or distracted demeanor, use a flatter tone of voice, and make it clear I am just going through the motions. Students see the difference easily, and they know why it matters: while both deliveries are the same on the surface, they convey opposing messages. In one, they see that I am using the ritual to do what it was designed to accomplish—that is, enable me to initiate a relationship with someone I have just met. In the other, it is clear that I have no genuine interest in getting the relationship off on the right foot.

We may understand this once again through the analogy of language. Lacking proper ritual, we have no common language by which to establish and manage social relationships. Just as I cannot communicate with someone if we do not speak the same language, without a common set of rituals, I do not know what signals my gestures are conveying to others and vice versa. However, even with a common language it is possible to use perfectly constructed sentences to tell lies, use irony, or be sarcastic. That is what the second handshake did—I used a ritual performance designed to express a desire to initiate a relationship to communicate just the opposite.

This is the meaning of *yi*, or "appropriateness." It is the quality of genuineness that motivates ritual behavior and makes it effective. In early literary Chinese, the word had multiple meanings, and its use in the *Analects* invited its readers to see more than one. The word could mean "rightness" in the sense of being proper and in accordance with a social standard. Confucian texts in following generations used it in this sense, and English translators have used the word "righteousness" to highlight this meaning. It also means "to signify." Combining these readings, we can understand *yi* as a kind of right signification, an inspiration of ritual actions with their proper meaning and purpose. A lack of appropriateness indicates hypocrisy, a misalignment between inner intention and outward expression, leading to nothing but a dead display. Confucius had no use for this, as seen in his exchange with the man who did not want to observe the standard three-year mourning period for his parents following their deaths. If observing the outward form of the ritual did not reflect genuine inner grief, then why go through the motions?

Thus, the combination of ritual propriety with appropriateness solved two potential impediments to social communication. A lack of ritual propriety (such as the outward form of the handshake) is tantamount to lacking a language. In that case, we may have a sincere desire to communicate genuine sentiments but will not have a channel through which to do so. On the other hand, a lack of appropriateness is like having a language but using it to lie. In either case, neither language nor ritual propriety can achieve its end. However, there is one other aspect of appropriateness that calls for our attention. Appropriateness keeps ritual propriety from becoming rigid and inflexible.

Confucius has often been presented as conservative or even reactionary. Rather than looking for new solutions to address the political turmoil of his age, he looked backward to a golden age when the first emperors of the Zhou dynasty ruled with ritual propriety and benevolence, and he thought the solution was to restore their practices. That is why he put so much effort into finding, restoring, and teaching from texts that preserved their ritual forms. However, Confucius showed flexibility as seen in the quotation at the head of this section where he displayed a willingness to adopt a deviation from the practices of the early Zhou by substituting silk caps for linen caps since the former are more economical. Here, it is appropriateness that justifies the change, as in other passages in the *Analects* Confucius decries extravagance. However, he rejects the new-fangled practice of bowing to the ruler after ascending the stairs to the dais because it is presumptuous and so violates appropriateness by encoding the wrong attitude.

Considerations of appropriateness may also justify breaking the rules of ritual propriety in certain situations. In the passage from the book of *Mencius* quoted above, a man proposes that since the rules dictate that a man may not physically touch a woman, then perhaps it would be improper to grasp his sister-in-law's hand to save her should she fall off a boat. Mencius rejects such reasoning, declaring that a man who would not save a drowning family member "is a wolf" (the comparison with an animal will prove more than just metaphorical, as we will see later). In another passage he says that even though it is appropriate for a vagrant to accept an offering of food, he would be justified in refusing it if it were offered with a curse and a blow. Appropriateness here would involve maintaining human dignity even if it meant going hungry. Such examples make clear that Confucius and his followers are not mere sticklers for proper ritual performance. Not only must ritual be infused with the right spirit in order to communicate its meaning and have its intended effect, but it can also be changed if and when a strictly by-the-book performance would actually have undesirable side effects such as unnecessary expense, offense against human dignity, or death. This steers a middle course between frequent and capricious changes to social practice and a rigorous conservatism that would rob them of human meaning.[2]

Once, many years ago, I was in an Episcopal church on a Sunday morning in North Carolina. The service featured a bishop visiting from another diocese as the guest preacher. During the opening hymn and procession, a young man was appointed the "bishop's chaplain"; his job was to walk in front of the bishop and carry his crozier, an ornate replica of a shepherd's crook that serves as a symbol of office. Abruptly, a man standing next to me stopped singing and whispered to me, "Look at that! The bishop's chaplain is carrying the crozier with the crook facing backward! Doesn't he know that you carry a visiting bishop's crozier with the crook facing forward and a resident bishop's crozier with the crook facing backward?" I could not help but think that this man had lost the forest for the trees. It may be that in the past, when a congregation was largely illiterate and could not just read an announcement in a printed bulletin, the direction of the crook signaled the identity of the bishop and thus served a purpose. In that situation, one should not lightly change the practice. However, nowadays it is unnecessary, and to cling to it as an unchanging rule subverts the role that the opening ritual plays in uniting people into a congregation and focusing their attention on the service. (By the way, I work with colleagues who specialize in liturgical history who have never heard of this rule.)

Appropriateness, therefore, both enables ritual to communicate and keeps it relevant. It prevents the use of ritual propriety for deception and unbending scrupulousness, both of which render ritual propriety futile.

THE CONFUCIAN SELF: PROCESSIVE AND POROUS

So far, we have not encountered any ideas that differ radically from Western concepts. Writers such as Thomas Jefferson and

Miss Manners have told English-speaking readers for a long time that ritual propriety ("etiquette," "protocol") serves the function of smoothing social relationships between people who do not already know each other by providing a set of stereotyped actions that assure others of our good intentions. The idea of hypocrisy is also nothing new, and it does not surprise us that even modern Mandarin uses the stock phrase *nei wai yi zhi* (the inner is consistent with the outer) to describe personal integrity and lack of guile. However, to really understand the Confucian sense of this congruence, we need to begin pondering some ideas about the self that are quite foreign to Western ways of thinking.

According to David Hall and Roger T. Ames, Western philosophy since the time of Plato and Aristotle has been "substantialist," which means that we believe that things are defined by their being, by what they *are*.[3] Most readers of this book probably do not consider themselves philosophers, but this way of thinking has seeped into the broader culture and colors the way we view ourselves, other selves, and what the word *self* means. We can see this in the way we typically think about hypocrisy. The word *hypocrisy* derives from the Greek term for the mask that actors wore on stage when performing a play. It covered their faces and only allowed the audience to see the character played and not the actor whose true face it covered. Thus, we see ourselves as having a true nature that is fixed, and the achievement of authenticity requires adjusting our outward presentation so that it faithfully represents this core self. We strive to "find out who we really are" with the intention of fashioning our public behaviors and personas so that they express this inner core. Failure to do so means we are wearing a mask and putting on an act. In essence, we all aspire to be Popeye the Sailor saying, "I yam what I yam!"

For Confucians, indeed for all early Chinese thought, things were understood not by what they *are* but by what they *do*. They have no solid, unchanging essence but are seen as events, happenings, doings, trajectories, behaviors, developments, actions. The self is *processive*. It is not an entity that can assume roles and identities; it *is* the enacting of roles itself. For example, in the West we can identify someone as a king even if he completely fails to carry out the duties and expectations of a king properly. For contrast, consider this dialogue from the book of *Mencius* regarding the assassination of ancient kings widely regarded as corrupt:

> 1B:15. King Xuan of Qi asked, "Is it true that [Emperor] Tang drove out [King] Jie and that [King] Wu put [King] Zhou to rout?" Mencius replied, "This is what has come down to us." The king said, "Then is it permitted that a minister murder his lord?" Mencius said, "One who robs humanity is deemed a bandit. He who robs righteousness is deemed a destroyer. Those who destroy and rob are considered merely men. I have heard of killing the mere man Zhou, but I have never heard that a lord was killed."

Notice that Mencius does not admit that Zhou, the last king of the Shang dynasty, was a bad king; his claim is that he was not a king at all. Since he was not doing what kings do, one could not use the word to describe him. Based on his actions, one could only refer to him as a "destroyer" or a "mere man." This differs significantly from Western thought in which Zhou could be called a king because he *was* the king, albeit a bad one.

We can see other instances of this in Confucian practices throughout history. In the West, we might think that ghosts are quite distinct from gods, but anthropologists and historians have recorded cases of ghosts attaining divine status because they stop doing what ghosts do (make trouble for people and haunt locations) and begin doing what gods do (accepting offerings and granting requests to people not related to them by blood). A family may remove an ancestor's memorial plaque from the home altar if the ancestor is not doing what ancestors do (protect the family from baleful spiritual influences). Conversely, a person who took you in as an orphan, educated you, arranged a suitable marriage, and helped you establish yourself in the world may get a spot on the ancestral altar after death because they did for you in life what blood relatives do. In all these cases, the behavior determined the status rather than any claim of an essential "identity."

We may even observe this in the structure of contemporary Mandarin. As a student of Chinese living in Taiwan in the early 1990s, I learned how to say, "I am a Buddhist" (*wo xin fo*), and "I am a vegetarian" (*wo chi su*). Later, as I became more aware of the Chinese habit of ignoring substance in favor of process, it struck me that the first sentence literally translates "I believe Buddhism," and the second, "I eat a vegetarian diet."[4] The verb *to be* does not occur in them, so they do not imply an identity but rather communicate a set of actions. I found this intriguing, and I adopted these ways of speaking to see what effect they might have. Consequently, nowadays I will say "I practice Buddhism" and "I stopped eating meat," and I find that expressing my meaning in this way is much less fraught than identifying as *a* Buddhist or *a* vegetarian. However, sometimes my interlocutor will ask, "Are you a vegetarian, then?" To make clear that I am not claiming this identity, I will respond, "No, I just stopped eating meat, that's all." In both instances I am indicating that I did not turn into something that I wasn't before. I merely made a behavioral change.

If I have pressed this point at some length, it is because Western culture cannot let go of the verb *to be* as the main way of identifying things, even when translating Confucian texts. In verse 12.11 of the *Analects*, we have this passage: "There is government, when the prince is prince, and the minister is minister; when the father is father, and the son is son." All the English translations I have examined phrase this passage in a similar way. The prince should *be* a prince, the minister should *be* a minister, and so forth. However, the Chinese text translated literally would read, "Prince, prince, minister minister, father father, son son" (*jun jun, chen chen, fu fu, zi zi*). The verb *to be* is nowhere to be found. Since ancient Chinese characters do not always have fixed grammatical functions, a closer translation might read, "Rulers *rule*; ministers *minister*; fathers *father*; sons *son*," where each phrase is a noun-verb pair. What do rulers do? They *rule*. What do ministers do? They *minister*, and so on.

Thus, nothing in the Confucian worldview simply is what it is. Their identification and status depend upon action and development, or, to use the Chinese term, its "way" (*dao*), a topic to which we will return later. Here, it is enough to say that this concept will impact the relationship Confucianism sees between our inner selves and our outward presentation, and more significantly, its ideas about being human.

The Confucian self is also porous, and this will affect the way in which the tradition sees the relationship between one person and another. The philosopher and social historian Charles Taylor describes the modern Western view of the self as enclosed, "bounded," or "buffered."[5] This means that we tend to see ourselves as encased within our own heads, and others have no access to our inner selves except when we choose to express them outwardly through our words, gestures, manner of dress, or other signals. This, Taylor says, is a recent shift that resulted from scientific developments in the modern world, and it superseded an earlier phase in which we saw possibilities for other beings to enter our minds and produce thoughts through dreams, divine inspiration, demon possession, and the magic of telepathy. The modern view of the enclosed self preserves our individuality and autonomy, and it makes us responsible for the degree to which others influence us.

The Confucian self is not so bounded. Not only are we more processes than objects but we are also mutually co-creative or co-directive. This is because as social beings, we do not simply occupy a unique space within our social networks from which we decide how to deal with others. We are more like nodes in that network, constantly reconfiguring as we interact with other nodes. I am a father only in relation to my children, and my performance of fatherhood shifts with each interaction with them. The same goes for my function as a son, a teacher, a citizen, a colleague, a friend, and for all the roles I manage alongside others. Even more deeply, however, it means that the very function and direction of my self proceeds under the influence of others. They affect who I am from moment to moment without any conscious direction from me. This does not mean I am under their control, because I am simultaneously impacting their direction. The point is that selves are not independent entities that experience change through interaction; they are always-emerging vectors that surge and flow in the very interactions themselves. We will see how this affects the Confucian way of construing the self and others below.

THE INNER AND THE OUTER

Analects 5.25
The Master said, "Fine words, an insinuating appearance, and excessive respect—Zuo Qiu Ming was ashamed of them. I also am ashamed of them. To conceal resentment against a person, and appear friendly with him—Zuo Qiu Ming was ashamed of such conduct. I also am ashamed of it."

Because it does not recognize a solid inner self, Confucianism pictures a relationship between the inner and outer aspects of a person that I have not encountered in Western thought. Confucians do not prioritize adjusting our outward presentation to reflect the inner self as we tend to do in the West. Instead, the relationship is dialectical, meaning that the inner and outer aspects of our selves influence and form each other. What would this mean in practice? Let's look at an example.

I once heard about a classical musician who was engaged to play Carnegie Hall. The usual practice in this situation is for men to wear a tuxedo while performing, but this musician did not want to. He said he just wasn't the kind of person who felt comfortable in a tuxedo, and he chose to wear a flannel shirt, jeans, and work boots instead. This would improve the performance because he would be presenting his authentic self to the audience; and at any rate, the music would be just as good, so it should not matter. After telling this story, I always stop and ask my students if they approve of this performer's decision to buck the tuxedo, and if not, do they at least understand the argument he is making? The answer is usually yes, though some will answer no to the first question.

Confucius would be appalled at such a stance. A classical concert in Carnegie Hall is a ritual situation, and ritual propriety calls for this performer to wear the tuxedo. To the objection that this feels inauthentic and smacks of hypocrisy, Confucius would reply that there is no unchanging inner self that requires that the outer display always conform to it. The outer display of our public face can actually work backward and alter the inner sense of self. Therefore, the performer *should wear the tuxedo*, even if it does not feel right. The expectation is that by wearing it consistently, one performance after another, this musician will become habituated to it and, in time, will *become a person who feels at home wearing a tuxedo.*

This runs contrary to Western expectations, but I have found it to be true in my own experience. In 1995, I accepted my first academic post and found myself now assuming the role of "the professor." It seemed clear to me that this was a social role with expectations attached to it, but I was not sure what they were. There were professors who appeared on newscasts as authority figures; there was the movie *The Absent-Minded Professor*, and there was the character of the Professor on the TV show *Gilligan's Island*, who seemed practically omniscient. Adding to the haze was the fact that I had been a student only a short while before. Consequently I did not know what the role entailed and how I should present myself in the classroom and in society at large.

The result was a mess. As I have already described above, I still identified with my students more than with my colleagues. I tried to be everyone's friend. I still dressed and acted more like one of the students and tried to ignore the fact that I was in a position of genuine authority with respect to them. As noted, the atmosphere in the classroom changed for the better once I decided to act the role of the professor and clarified role expectations and boundaries. But here I can add another effect of this transition: over time, the outward presentation *did* sink in and alter my inner sense of self. During my earlier days, I told people that I just wasn't the kind of person who felt comfortable in a coat and a tie. However, after deciding to honor the role I occupied and the ritual of the classroom, I gradually changed, and wearing more formal clothes than my students and presenting the persona of a professor came to feel more and more natural. These days, I own it pretty well and feel no unease or lack of authenticity in it. We might call this an instance of "fake it 'til you make it," but the inner change seems genuine to me.

SELF AND OTHER

Analects 1.8

The Master said, "If the scholar be not grave, he will not call forth any veneration, and his learning will not be solid. Hold faithfulness and sincerity as first principles. Have no friends not equal to yourself. When you have faults, do not fear to abandon them."

Analects 1.14

The Master said, "He who aims to be a man of complete virtue in his food does not seek to gratify his appetite, nor in his dwelling place does he seek the appliances of ease; he is earnest in what he is doing, and careful in his speech; he frequents the company of men of principle that he may be rectified—such a person may be said indeed to love to learn."

Analects 15.5

The Master said, "May not Shun be instanced as having governed efficiently without exertion? What did he do? He did nothing but gravely and reverently occupy his royal seat [facing south]."

Mencius 1A.1

Mencius went to see King Hui of Liang. The king said, "Sir, you traveled a thousand *li* to come here as if it were not far. What do you bring that will profit my state?" Mencius answered, "Why must Your Majesty say 'profit'? Humanity and righteousness are all that I bring. When a ruler says, 'What can profit my state?' then the nobles will ask, 'What will profit my house?' and the knights and commoners will ask, 'What will profit me personally?' Those above and those below will strive against each other for their own advantage and put the state at risk."

As we saw above, the Confucian self is not only processive but also porous. This means that we are radically open to other people. We do not simply listen to them from within an enclosed self and then decide whether to adapt or make personal changes; other people enter into our selves and changes simply happen, sometimes without our awareness. Thus, Confucius and his disciples stressed that one ought to choose one's companions with care as seen in the first two extracts above, because our associates can alter our behavior by their mere proximity to us. Your parents may have told you the same thing. They knew the power of association with good or bad people in molding character.

This is the point of Mencius's admonition in the fourth citation. He managed to get an audience with King Hui of Liang, and the first question the king put to him was about actions that could profit his kingdom. Mencius demurs on this question, saying he offers only the Confucian teachings of humanity (*ren*) and righteousness (*yi*). If the king only pursues profit and advantage, then his own advisers and high officials will absorb that pattern from him and will display it in seeking profit for their own families; and below them, local officials and commoners will seek only profit for themselves. The fabric of the kingdom will fall apart as everyone scrambles to look after themselves.

In contrast, Confucius points out that the legendary sage-emperor Shun took no overt actions[6] to govern but simply "faced south." In a traditional Chinese court, the emperor's throne occupied the north end of the hall, and so when seated there, the emperor faced south with court officials divided into eastern and western ranks on either side. The sense of this passage, then, is that Shun simply placed himself in the correct ritual position and things took care of themselves. How? Because his ritual propriety diffused out to his courtiers, through them to their families and home districts, and from there to the common people. This did not happen because autonomous human beings noted his good example and rationally decided to emulate him. It was a kind of outward spreading "infection" of virtue that helped to cement his society together and inspire everyone to do their part for the common good. This is in stark contrast to the behavior Mencius predicts King Hui's subjects would display if he were to show only an interest in profit.

Another early Confucian text, the *Great Learning* (*Daxue*), mapped out this process with greater precision, detailing eight steps that lead from personal development to successful governance and world peace:

(1) Things being investigated, knowledge became complete. (2) Their knowledge being complete, their thoughts were sincere. (3) Their thoughts being sincere, their hearts were then rectified. (4) Their hearts being rectified, their persons were cultivated. (5) Their persons being cultivated, their families were regulated. (6) Their families being regulated, their states were rightly governed. (7) Their states being rightly governed, (8) the whole [world] was made tranquil and happy.[7]

This passage was highly influential in the later development of Confucian thought, and many subsequent authors used it to weave theories of the relationship of the individual to society. We will have occasion to examine these later. For now, let us simply note that it counsels the reader to begin with personal cultivation starting with study (investigating things to extend knowledge) that will have a beneficial effect on the individual (leading to making the will sincere and further personal cultivation). This means that study is not simply for the accumulation of facts for the improvement of the person; even in modern Mandarin we find the expression "study to put into practice" (*xue yi zhi yong*). The last four steps show the outward radiation of virtue as successful personal moral cultivation leads to proper family life, benevolent government in the student's country, and finally to world peace. All of this happens because the student takes it upon himself or herself to become a beneficial force acting on the selves within his or her orbit. It happens naturally because we permeate one another.

I verified this for myself the hard way. Many years ago, I went for a year of intensive language study at National Taiwan University in Taipei. When I arrived, I found myself surrounded by fellow students from many other universities whose motivations for studying Mandarin varied greatly. As is usual in such situations, I needed to create a social network so I would have friends to take meals with, converse, and explore the city. I fell in with a small group of other students who turned out to hold values quite different from mine that came out in behaviors and conversation I found unacceptable. The longer I associated with them, the more I found myself unwittingly veering into their ways of speaking and acting, and the only remedy in the end was to find other students to spend time with. As I reflected on this later, I saw that it was happening just as the Confucian texts (and my mother) had predicted. I never made any conscious decision to emulate them; it just seemed to happen as if by absorption. Thus, Confucius was right in maintaining that, at least in the early stages, one should be cautious about picking friends. Their ethos and morals will seep into the porous self and alter the course of its development.

BRINGING TOGETHER RITUAL, APPROPRIATENESS, AND THE INTERACTIVE SELF

In sum, the Confucian self is not the enclosed, autonomous, and rational individual valued in Western culture. There is no core self such that acting outwardly in a way that expresses it is authentic, while acting in a way that conceals it is hypocritical. Rather, the inner self is a process that we can redirect toward or away from ritual propriety, and adjusting our outward behavior to reflect proper decorum will work inward to adjust our inner self's vector. By assuming the ritual propriety expected of a professor in the classroom, I eventually *became* the professor. In addition, the self is porous, not enclosed. Our social selves overlap and exert mutual influence such that others can affect our growth and development merely through prolonged proximity. Thus, we must keep our distance from bad company during our early cultivation, and the hoped-for result of successful cultivation will be that we exert a positive influence on those within our orbit. Applied throughout society, this favorable influence will spread beyond our immediate family and circle of associates to the nation and the world.

The cultivation of ritual propriety and appropriateness constitutes a path that one follows. The dynamic concept of the path or the Way offers further contrasts to ordinary Western thought, and so we will explore it in the next chapter.

3

THE WAY (*DAO*)
道

In the opening scenes of the movie *Crouching Tiger, Hidden Dragon*, we see Master Li Mu Bai (played by Chow Yun-fat) and Yu Shu Lien (played by Michelle Yeoh) talking about an experience that Master Li had while meditating in a Buddhist monastery. He describes a vision of ineffable light and wonders why his meditation teacher had never spoken to him about it. If you watch the movie in its English dub or follow the English subtitles, you will think that Shu Lien asks him if he "was enlightened." However, in the Mandarin version, she asks him if he "attained the Way" (*de dao*), an expression by which virtually all Chinese religions designate the goal of practice. In this chapter, we will see that this way of thinking about the purpose of self-cultivation differs markedly from Western ways of thinking.

What is the "Way"? Here we are very fortunate. This is a rare case in which an English word captures much of the meaning of the Chinese original. *Way* has the same basic meaning and can spin out into the same extended or metaphorical meanings as the Chinese *dao*. We can break this down into three layers:

First, both *dao* and *way* mean a path or road as a physical ribbon of sand, gravel, concrete, or asphalt upon which we walk or drive vehicles. It retains this sense in modern Mandarin: *Daolu* means "road"; *renxing dao* means "sidewalk" (a "*dao* on which people walk"); and *danxing dao* means a "one-way street" (a "*dao* for traveling in a single direction"). Often an English street name will end with the word *way*.

Second, extrapolating from the physical road or path, *way* can mean a set of directions for getting from one place to another. We can ask about the best way to get from our present location to our destination. Here we have moved the discussion from the paths themselves to the act of traveling along those paths.

Third, at a further level of abstraction we can use *way* to speak about any goal-oriented activity not involving actual travel along physical pathways. My students may ask me about the best way to prepare for an exam, my graduate students might seek advice on the best way to prepare for the academic job market, or we might ask about the optimum way to structure our finances.

The Confucian *dao* works at this level. Throughout Confucian texts, we see several goals articulated: prosperity, increasing the population, peace, order, love, and respect. The *dao* of Confucianism, therefore, is the "way" to achieve these goals. If we bear this in mind, much of what is said in this chapter will make more sense. (On a side note, other religions such as Chinese Buddhism and Daoism take the word *dao* to further heights of meaning, often very poetic, metaphorical, and even metaphysical. These usages will not concern us here.)

We will now look at the Confucian Way from three angles. First, we will briefly look at Herbert Fingarette's claim that it is a "way without a crossroads." Next, we will see that it is a way without a destination. Finally, we will see that it is a human way, requiring no input from spirits or gods.

A WAY WITHOUT A CROSSROADS

Mencius 4A.2

Confucius said, "There are only two Ways: Humanity and in-humanity."

In the modern world, most urban societies are multicultural and multilingual, giving us opportunities to see and compare several different ways of life and communication. Many are also religiously diverse, and we value the freedom to choose our own path from among several options. To say that Confucianism is a way without a crossroads, then, can be a little off-putting to modern sensibilities. Herbert Fingarette suggested this interpretation, so we will first see what he meant and then see what we can make of it.[1]

Fingarette begins by pointing out that none of the discussions of the Way in the *Analects* includes the idea of free choice. As he puts it, path imagery can be elaborated to include the image of a crossroads quite easily, and yet the *Analects* never puts such an image forth. One is either on the Way or one is not; the text provides no way to think about options among which one may select. The reason, he says, is that the Confucian Way does not lead one to a destination but to a "condition," that of the person capable of navigating human relationships in such a way that he or she contributes to the flourishing and harmony of society.

Confucius did not insist that there was only one set of practices that led to this condition. In the passage given in the previous chapter, he notes that it is a matter of indifference whether one wears a linen cap or a silk cap when appearing before the throne. In a similar way, we may observe that there are certainly other ways besides a handshake to initiate a relationship. In other cultures, one may bow, kiss on the cheeks, or perform other actions. All these can serve the purpose of providing a means of communicating one's good intentions. As human social groups form, conventional behaviors will emerge and take hold, and in time they will be codified as the "right way" to get things done.

Thus, to say the Way in Confucianism lacks a crossroads does not imply that there is only one proper way to do things any more than we could say only one of the languages spoken throughout the world is the "right" one, while all the others are wrong. Rather than the specific form that ritual propriety takes, the Way is found in the intention itself, and here there are only two alternatives: one has the intention to form a harmonious society with others or one does not. Before we can commence on any program of Confucian self-cultivation, we must want the result it aims at. The unfolding of this desire in the daily interactions between people will then produce forms that bring it to realization: the handshake, the funeral, the gift, and so on. If we lack this desire, the Way will not manifest, and human relationships will be lost in confusion. There is no alternative to the Way seen in this light, and thus no crossroads presenting rational options. That is why Mencius quotes Confucius as saying there is only humanity and inhumanity.

This helps to allay a misgiving that modern society may have about this Way. It may seem that Confucius envisioned this ideal for a fairly uniform community, one in which the social practices and morals that form ritual propriety do not vary. It might thus seem ill-suited for a modern, urban, multicultural setting. It may be easy for us to imagine that he intended for political authorities, assisted by ritual specialists, to impose a single set of practices. The fact that he spent a great deal of time seeking out literary sources for the reconstruction of early Zhou dynasty practices only reinforces this impression.

However, let us keep two things in mind: First, Confucianism does not recognize autonomous, enclosed selves upon which social norms must be inscribed or enforced but rather the "porous self" described in the previous chapter. Human beings influence one another's behaviors and attitudes as they live side by side, and it can happen spontaneously, without any conscious planning or external imposition. Second, as just noted, the Way is not fundamentally a specific set of prescriptions but rather a basic desire to form community with others. In this scenario, communities that come into prolonged contact, however distinct they might be at the outset, will begin to converge as overlapping selves exercise mutual influence.

Certain adaptations will take place almost immediately out of necessity. It would be impractical, unsafe, and physically impossible for a community moving to the United States from a country where the custom is to drive on the left side of the road to insist that this is a deeply held part of their culture that they wish to maintain. Other aspects of the neighboring communities will change more or less slowly, such as social conventions like the handshake. The final result is that they eventually merge until one cannot tell them apart, just as one cannot distinguish descendants of the ancient Anglo-Saxons from their Norman French conquerors in contemporary England. While we cannot ignore the often fraught histories between different populations that instill a sense of separateness, Confucianism invites us to acknowledge the countervailing human drive to form viable communities, something that requires a convergence of the rituals and customs by which we regulate our common lives.

The point here is not to argue against multiculturalism and its benefits and challenges. Rather, Confucius reminds us of the dynamism of human social life and suggests that the desire to build sustainable lives together is built into us and naturally seeks ways to self-fulfillment.

A WAY WITHOUT A DESTINATION

Analects 2.4

The Master said, "At fifteen, I had my mind bent on learning. At thirty, I stood firm. At forty, I had no doubts. At fifty, I knew the decrees of Heaven. At sixty, my ear was an obedient organ for the reception of truth. At seventy, I could follow what my heart desired, without transgressing what was right."

Analects 8.7

The philosopher Zeng said, "The officer may not be without breadth of mind and vigorous endurance. His burden is heavy and his course is long. [Humanity] is the burden which he considers it is his to sustain—is it not heavy? Only with death does his course stop—is it not long?"

Analects 6.29

The Master said, "Perfect is the virtue which is according to the Constant Mean! Rare for a long time has been its practice among the people."

Analects 7.34

The Master said, "The sage and the man of [humanity]—how dare I rank myself with them? That I strive to become such without satiety, and teach others without weariness—this much can be said of me." Gong Xi Hua said, "This is just what we, the disciples, cannot imitate you in."

Analects 8.13

The Master said, "With sincere faith he unites the love of learning; holding firm to death, he is perfecting the excellence of his course."

Many religious and ethical traditions of the world, regardless of whether they see human beings in processive terms (like Buddhism) or substantialist terms (such as Christianity), put people on a road that leads somewhere. In Buddhism and some forms of Hinduism, the goal lies at the end of a long program of study and training, and it consists in liberation from reincarnation and transformation into a new state of being. In Christianity, one may cross the "finish line" at the very beginning of the journey as one accepts salvation by means of Jesus Christ's sacrifice and resurrection. Crossing this finish line signals the end of one form of life and the beginning of another. In the example of Buddhism, this means that one puts aside the practices that led to enlightenment and liberation as they are no longer needed. Just as one who has landed their boat on the shore does not pick it up and carry it inland, so a buddha no longer engages in the cultivation that brought him to buddhahood. The Christian becomes a "new creature" and leaves their old way of life behind while moving forward in gratitude.

The Confucian tradition differs from these others in this respect. As seen above, the goal is not to follow a path until you reach a destination. To "attain the Way" simply means to get yourself on the path and to keep on it, always oriented in the right direction and always moving forward. This helps us understand why Confucius very rarely identified anyone—whether his disciples, his contemporaries, historical figures, or even himself—as having attained the final goal. To do so would be to declare that they had achieved moral self-perfection and had no further need of practice. In *Analects* 1.4, the disciple Zengzi says that every day he examines his conscience to see whether he did his best on behalf of others, whether he was trustworthy in dealing with his friends, and whether he only taught moral lessons that he himself lived by. The tradition presumes that he will do so every evening of his life; at no point will he claim that he has perfected himself in these areas and has no further need for self-critique.

Furthermore, Confucius's autobiographical poem quoted above shows that the Master himself not only kept at his studies all his life (he died at age seventy-three) but that he made continual progress and reached new milestones right to the end. He sets his heart-mind[2] on learning at fifteen, an age when educated young men would already have been in school for many years. At this age he seems to have declared it his vocation. In *Analects* 7.17 he asks for a few more years of life, feeling that there are levels of study that he would only be able to undertake once he reaches the age of fifty. This seems to indicate that he had some idea of life stages, with certain areas of learning appropriate for certain ages. Only by age seventy does he believe that he has internalized the lessons of his studies so deeply that he no longer experiences temptations to deviate from the Way. As Zengzi says, "His road ends only with death."

This may strike you as very prosaic and uncontroversial. After all, we will live in human society to the end of our lives and will always need to pay attention to interpersonal matters. However, I remember that as a young man, I thought of the ordinary doings of daily life as a mere backdrop to the more important aims of religious transformation. I attended to family relations, educational pursuits, and getting along with colleagues at work, but this was all part of what Christians might call "the world" and Buddhists "samsara." The serious task of self-cultivation aimed at a transformative experience—call it enlightenment or the beatific vision—that would take me out of all these pedestrian pursuits and show me realms of meaning beyond.

Confucius calls his students to focus all their efforts at self-cultivation on the details of daily life, work, and relationships. In the third quotation above, the phrase "the Constant Mean" translates the two Chinese characters *zhongyong*, where *zhong* means "center," "equilibrium," or "to balance," while *yong* can mean "the ordinary, the everyday" or "the constant." The point of this passage is that humankind has no greater aim than to find and keep equilibrium while attending to the everyday. We should not read this in a Zen sense, taking it to mean finding the extraordinary or seeing our buddha-nature while "chopping wood and carrying water" but to concentrate on daily realities simply to get them right. Every day we refine ourselves in ritual propriety animated by appropriateness so as to maintain equilibrium in ourselves and in others. We never arrive at perfection; we simply keep at it until the end. For Confucius, there is no higher calling than this.

In my experience, teaching Western students that the Confucian Way has no crossroads and no destination raises no special difficulties and produces no resistance. These aspects of the Way may be thought-provoking but not too startling. It was when we got to this path as a human way that resistance appeared.

A HUMAN WAY

Analects 15.29
The Master said, "A man can enlarge the [Way]; [the Way can] not enlarge the man."

"So, if everyone agreed that it is all right to eat babies, then eating babies is all right?" This is perhaps the most provocative question a student has ever asked in class, and it was prompted by my introduction of the idea that the Way in Confucianism is a human way. While he posed the question in an extreme manner, it was not the first or only time this aspect of Confucian thought had aroused concern. Confucian humanism evokes a reflexive fear of moral relativism in Western culture. Put simply, if there is no moral authority outside of the human community, then what is to stop people from agreeing that anything, even something so despicable as eating babies, is acceptable, and why would they not go ahead and do it free of guilt? Surely wayward and fallible human beings need a divine authority to set reliable and consistent standards.

And yet Confucian societies have never fallen into such behaviors. Even Catholic missionaries in China in the late sixteenth century admired Confucian ethics so much that in their letters home they described the Sage as someone who must have had a natural grasp of God's law. We will attempt a different way of understanding the issues here, and it will require us to examine two factors: the collective production of social mores, and the goal-orientation of human conventions. The first will lead us to see that Western individualism prevents us from seeing a possible source of moral reasoning, and the second will account for why human-created ethics do not veer into horrific practices. In each case, the analogy with language will serve us once again.

First, then, let us try to discern the feature of Western culture that mainly leads to the fear of relativism and the student's pointed question. We tend to see no higher source of moral authority than the autonomous individual, free to decide on their own what standards will govern their behavior. The specter of relativism arises because we see no other source of moral reasoning. If all individuals are independent and equal, then no one can set standards for anyone else. At a higher level, no community can dictate the mores of another. We respond to others' admonitions with "That's just your opinion; it doesn't apply to me" or "Your community has nothing to say to mine." We believe that common standards can only come about through free agreement, coercion, material inducement, or other means besides authority. The most widespread remedy for relativism in the West has been to take moral authority out of the hands of human beings altogether and impute it to an omniscient lawgiver who stands over humankind. Even if everyone in a given society decides there is nothing wrong with eating babies, this transcendent moral authority will still say otherwise, and human beings get a reliable moral compass that does not wobble due to human willfulness.

Confucianism raises the prospect that between the free individual and God there is another actor, a possible third arbiter of social practices: the community of human beings itself, composed of but not reducible to individual actors. Language provides a helpful analogy here. I have not yet found anyone willing to claim that the English language came down from God and that to violate the rules of grammar constitutes a sin. It arises within human communities through a long collective process of trial and error, beginning with almost random sounds and gestures and being refined along the way by people as they used it until it evolved into the nuanced medium of communication that it is today. Even now, if we are attentive to the use of English in modern society, we can still hear experimentation and innovation taking place, signaling further evolution to come.

Even though everyone acknowledges that it is a purely human production, no one dismisses English as "merely subjective" or makes a claim that there is no standard binding on the community of speakers. Quite the opposite; we spend a vast amount of time, effort, and resources in educating children and students in "proper English." The reason is that language does not arise from the activity of isolated individuals, each one bearing equal authority. It is a collective production, ongoingly maintained and adjusted by the community through countless acts of speech. No one person can make alterations, something I have illustrated over the years by trying to enlist students in a project to call the moving sidewalks in airports "slidewalks." It has not worked yet because the community of English speakers has not adopted the practice.

Confucian morality is likewise a collective production. It is not the case that individuals decide on their own to abide by a "social contract." (As some philosophers have pointed out, this cannot have happened because the idea of "contract" would have already had to be in place.) People live together, and we have already seen that the "porous" nature of the Confucian self means that they influence one another in subtle ways. Like language, conventions of acceptable behavior arise in the process of living together, and the standard that emerges—and keeps emerging through the daily interactions of common life—cannot be trivialized as merely subjective or dismissed as not applying to individuals who choose to ignore it. If you would like to see this principle in action, you may repeat an experiment that several college friends and I once tried. At your next spaghetti dinner, put aside your cutlery and eat with your hands. You will soon find that your outraged dinner companions will not be sympathetic to protests that their rules of ritual propriety do not apply to you just because they say so.

This shows that in Confucianism there is another moral source besides the two that Western culture recognizes. In between individuals and God there is the community, now understood as an actor in its own right, collectively producing social morals and practices. However, this still leaves a question dangling: If an entire society comes to believe it is acceptable to eat babies, then why wouldn't it be? To answer this, we need to look at the second proposition given above: Social mores are not random. They have a purpose, and those that fulfill the purpose will be retained, while those that do not will be abandoned. Let us return to the analogy of language. How does language settle into meaningful forms and not continue as a string of sounds without any pattern?

Language has a purpose, which is to communicate. Thus, while living languages constantly change in the course of daily use, not all variations survive. An example of a successful adaptation in English might be to clarify a phrase such as "the right house," which might mean either the correct house or the house on the right. By saying "the righthand house," you make your meaning clear. While an individual may at one time or another have used this phrase for the first time, it became part of the language only after the rest of the community saw how useful it was in improving communication and adopted it. Individuals may at other times invent new ways of saying things that the language community declines to adopt simply because no one sees any benefit in them. Because developments in language proceed only as they help language serve its purpose, the direction of change is not arbitrary or capricious but goal oriented. Social mores and practices also serve a purpose, which is the creation and maintenance of a harmonious society, one whose practices lead to trust and cooperation. In the Confucian view, the human community has sufficient authority to set rules and establish practices because, in the end, it is the community and not independent actors that decides to adopt or not adopt any given change.

This leaves room for variation. Just as we encounter an astonishing variety of languages on Earth, we can also see cultural differences that serve the purpose of creating a flourishing community equally well. The ritual of the handshake works to signal a desire to initiate a friendly relationship, but other communities have other rituals that serve equally well. This contrasts with Western modes of establishing boundaries. If we exclude the community as a separate source of social morality and see only capricious individuals who need their morals handed down from a divine lawgiver to live together, then the morality it adopts will lack flexibility. A human community can come to realize that a social practice does not serve it well and make adjustments, but a divinely ordained law is not so easily altered. Later Confucians noted this difference with Western Christianity and asserted the superiority of their humanistic way. In a 1643 anti-Jesuit work titled *Collected Refutations of Heterodoxy* (*Pixieji*), the Buddhist monk Ouyi Zhixu (1599–1655) said,

> Now let us suppose that prior to the division of Heaven and Earth there was one who was most spiritual and holy called the Lord of Heaven. Such a being would have the power to govern and there would be no disorder; he would be good and there would be no evil. Also, why [would there be any need to] wait for subsequent powers of spirits or philosophies of sages to trim, complete, or supplement its features? People also would not "combine their virtue with [that of] Heaven and Earth" or "precede Heaven and yet Heaven is not contrary to him." How could they know that we Confucians are the line that "continues Heaven['s teaching] and establishes morals"?[3]

For Zhixu, the Jesuit teaching of a God who hands down the Ten Commandments calls humans to mere obedience and nothing more. In contrast, the Confucian Way gives dignity to human beings by calling forth their creativity and judgment to cooperate with the natural world to establish and maintain the basic framework of human relationships. This not only gives the human Way of Confucianism much more flexibility and adaptability but also confers more significance on human life by giving people the chance to set their own course.

Here is an illustration that I have used in class: On the east side of our campus there is a metro station. As you exit the side gate and cross the street, you encounter a sidewalk that curves around through a patch of lawn to get to the station entrance. Alongside that sidewalk is a path through the grass that cuts across the curve and goes directly to the entrance. The sidewalk is analogous to Western individualistic-theistic morality: it was placed there by an authority who expected pedestrians to stay on it. The path through the grass illustrates the quotation from the *Analects* above declaring that people enlarge the Way, not vice versa. The path was not planned by anyone in authority. It appeared simply because people walked that way, and its location was determined by the fact that it traced the quickest route to the station entrance. As people walked, the path appeared spontaneously, but once it appeared, it had a power to draw people in to walk upon it.

We can now return to the question that opened this section: If a whole community were to decide that it is all right to eat babies, then is it all right? Absent a law-giving God to say it is not, then on what basis could anyone critique this practice? Does the question resist an answer that might be binding on people because we have been reduced to a radical moral relativism in which no one's moral precepts are better than anyone else's?

The way to approach the question from a Confucian perspective, I have found, is not to answer it but to pose a counterquestion. Suppose a society adopted such a practice, and its members routinely abducted and ate one another's children. How long would such a society last? Is that practice sustainable? It is very likely that due to the anger, thirst for revenge, and erosion of trust that would surely follow, that society would either self-correct or collapse in a fairly short time. Confucian texts recognize that human communities can and do fall into aberrant practices, and they give advice on what the Confucian student should do in response. These responses show that, even as a human product, the Way commands authority. History records Confucian martyrs who courageously criticized emperors in court for deviating from the Way of the Ancient Kings and paid for their witness with their lives.

THE LESSONS

In studying the Confucian Way, I came to understand several things I had not seen before. Considering it as a "Way without a crossroads" meant I had to pay attention to the human need to coalesce around a set of coherent social practices and the natural, almost unconscious way in which it happens even when we want to preserve differences. Details may differ, but the drive to form community abides, leaving self-isolation as the only alternative. Understanding it as a Way without a destination alerted me that life in human society demands constant attention, both to ourselves and to others. We are never dispensed from this task, although as Confucius attests, it can become easier as we get older. Finally, considering the path as a human Way caused me to think long and hard about the Western discourse of individualism and the way it blinds us to the action of the community as a distinct fountainhead of moral teaching. Our own cultural tendency to overlook this source gives rise to a need to locate moral authority outside the realm of human community and instills a groundless fear that relativism and chaos inevitably follow when human beings are left to establish their own structures and practices. I came to see the possibility that leaving the human community to take care of its own affairs can just as well call forth creativity and dignity as people take up the responsibility of learning how to get along.

4

THE PRINCELY MAN, THE SAGE, SINCERITY, AND HUMANITY

Analects 3.3

The Master said, "If a man be without [humanity], what has he to do with the rites of propriety? If a man be without [humanity], what has he to do with music?"

Once someone has "attained the Way" and is heading in the right direction, where do they go? If the Way truly has no ultimate destination, then how do we talk about the goal of self-cultivation? Confucianism does indeed set a goal in front of those who have attained the Way, but it is a constantly receding goal, one that the practitioner will never reach. This does not diminish its purpose, however. The goal serves as a marker, something that remains in front of us and keeps us oriented. Early Confucian texts use two nouns and two adjectives to illuminate this goal from different angles. The two nouns are "the princely man" (*junzi*) and "the sage" (*sheng*). The two adjectives are "sincerity" (*cheng*) and "humanity" (*ren*).

君子
THE PRINCELY MAN

Analects 1.14
The Master said, "He who aims to be a [princely man] in his food does not seek to gratify his appetite, nor in his dwelling place does he seek the appliances of ease; he is earnest in what he is doing, and careful in his speech; he frequents the company of men of principle that he may be rectified—such a person may be said indeed to love to learn."

Analects 6.18
The Master said, "Where the solid qualities are in excess of accomplishments, we have rusticity; where the accomplishments are in excess of the solid qualities, we have the manners of a clerk. When the accomplishments and solid qualities are equally blended, we then have the [princely man]."

Analects 7.33
The Master said, "In letters I am perhaps equal to other men, but the character of the [princely man], carrying out in his conduct what he professes, is what I have not yet attained to."

Analects 9.2
A man of the village of Da Xiang said, "Great indeed is [Confucius]! His learning is extensive, and yet he does not render his name famous by any particular thing." The Master heard the observation and said to his disciples, "What shall I practice? Shall I practice charioteering, or shall I practice archery? I will practice charioteering."

Analects 12.4

Sima Niu asked about the [princely man]. The Master said, "The [princely man] has neither anxiety nor fear." Niu said, "Being without anxiety or fear! Does this constitute what we call the [princely man]?" The Master said, "When internal examination discovers nothing wrong, what is there to be anxious about, what is there to fear?"

Translators have dealt with the Confucian term *junzi* in various ways: "princely man," "gentleman," "superior man," "man of complete virtue," "exemplary person," "higher type of man," "accomplished scholar," and so on. I choose "princely man" as most useful for our discussion, not in spite of the term's political overtones and male-centeredness but *because* of these qualities. It will help us to remember to whom Confucius primarily directed his remarks. As seen in chapter 1, Confucius aspired to a high position in government, one in which he would have enough authority and influence to affect the formulation and implementation of policy. Failing that, he took in students on the understanding that no matter their social background, he could teach them the skills and moral temperament they would need to ascend to such a position. Thus, we should bear in mind that his teachings were aimed almost exclusively at young men who sought government positions. It was in this context that he chose a term to sum up the intended result of his educational program.

At the time, the word *junzi* meant a person in such a position. We have already seen the word *jun* in the phrase usually (mis)translated as "Let the prince be a prince"; and the suffix -*zi* can mean "son of." (A common epithet for the emperor of China was *tianzi*, or "Son of Heaven.") Thus, *junzi* could mean "prince." However, by Confucius's day it also applied to men who occupied the kind of position of power and influence that Confucius sought, and it is even used in this sense in some parts of the *Analects*, such as 1:8, where Annping Chin translated the term "man of position."[1] However, elite society would not have applied this term to Confucius or his students. The class from which Confucius came was the *ru*, educated men who sought positions at court that rarely wielded decision-making power. They might also be referred to as *shi*, a word that is sometimes translated as "knight," "guard," "educated professional," and other such terms. It is telling that in *Analects* 13.20, Confucius makes an explicit distinction between a *shi* and a *junzi*, saying that the former serves the latter.

This raises a question: Why would Confucius choose a term that did not, and most probably would never, apply to him or his students to describe the ideal toward which he wanted them to aim? This may express a wistful dream that the men who exercised authority over the lands of the Zhou empire might attain their positions through merit instead of the usual means of gaining power: inheritance, rebellion, bribery, intrigue, and assassination. In his day, "men of position" did not usually gain their power through merit, though a few seem to have. *Shi*, by contrast, were hired into their positions based on their qualifications.

Against this, Confucius wondered: What if the rulers of states gained their power through virtue? There were models from the past in the texts Confucius had his students read. The sage-emperor Yao ceded his throne to the sage-emperor Shun, passing over his own son. Shun did the same in passing his throne to Yu the Great, the founder of the Xia dynasty who had demonstrated extraordinary diligence in working for the good of the common people justly and impartially. These precedents showed that a virtuous ruler could seek out a worthy successor for the good of the state and not automatically let it go to his son.

In the realpolitik of his day, this was no doubt a pipe dream. Rulers were pragmatists who knew how to operate the levers of power; lacking this ability, they rapidly fell to the next man of ambition. When Confucius held up the "princely man" as an ideal before his students, he was expressing his hope that they could become "men of position" themselves. Even if they could not become the ruler of a state, they might rise high enough in the ranks to be court advisers whose counsel could sway a ruler in the direction of virtue and benevolence. Perhaps as tutors to the royal heirs they could even help to raise up a new generation of enlightened rulers. But it was also a statement on the nature of rulership, which I have compressed into the maxim "the true ruler is formed, not born."

As time went on, Confucius's improbable dream of enlightened rulership made headway in Chinese governmental practice. During his day, most court advisers were handpicked by the ruler, and the emperor gave away fiefs to his allies, ennobling them into a hereditary aristocracy. Starting in the Han dynasty, however, a few men were selected for the highest posts in government by being presented to the throne as men of education and discernment, and the emperor quizzed them on policy questions to see how they thought. Over time, this developed into a civil examination system whose contents came from the Confucian classics. By the Ming and Qing dynasties (fourteenth to twentieth centuries), the examination system became the standard path into government, and the only hereditary figure left on the scene was the emperor himself. The dream of a government populated by properly formed men became a reality in a system that proved durable enough to last for centuries, until the moribund Qing ruling house suspended it in 1905. The examination system may not have always reliably produced "princely men," but it marked an advance over the old system.

We may see in this a parallel to the dreams of the educated classes in other parts of the world. The global North has largely abandoned hereditary rulership and enfeoffment of cronies as the accepted means of populating government in favor of other systems. This shift springs from the hope that the people who occupy the highest positions may, like Confucius and his disciples, be men and women who have received the kind of broad humanistic education that enables them to function in many different capacities. In our own way, we in the West maintain the distinction between a *shi* and a *junzi* in government. We may consider the former as the technocrats who occupy their positions through specific qualifications. I imagine that with my language training and educational focus on East Asia, I might have gone to work for the US Department of State and spent my career as a China specialist, rising from one rank to another within that narrow track.

But compare this credential-based career path with that followed by someone like George H. W. Bush (1924–2018). He embodied qualities that suited him to many high-level posts in very different places: head of a major corporation, director of the CIA, ambassador to China, ambassador to the United Nations, congressman from Texas, vice president, and president of the United States. This may well represent what Confucius meant when he hoped his students could become *junzi*. Their knowledge of history and ritual, their memorization of selected poems, their appreciation of music, and their practical experience would prepare them for the kind of "plug and play" career that Bush had, one in which they could be entrusted with high office in almost any capacity because of their temperament and vision. Leaving the technical details to the *shi* working underneath them, they could direct any government agency entrusted to them guided by virtue and a view of the big picture.

聖
THE SAGE

Analects 2.1
The Master said, "He who exercises government by means of his virtue may be compared to the north polar star, which keeps its place and all the stars turn toward it."

Analects 7.26
The Master said, "A sage it is not mine to see; could I see a [princely man], that would satisfy me." The Master said, "A good man it is not mine to see; could I see a man possessed of constancy, that would satisfy me."

Analects 8.19
The Master said, "Great indeed was Yao as a sovereign! How majestic was he! It is only Heaven that is grand, and only Yao corresponded to it. How vast was his virtue! The people could find no name for it. How majestic was he in the works which he accomplished! How glorious in the elegant regulations which he instituted!"

Mencius 4B.32
Mencius said, "How would I differ from others? Were not Yao and Shun the same as others?"

Xunzi 2.10
Ritual serves to rectify the person; the teacher serves to rectify the ritual. How would persons rectify themselves without ritual? How would one identify the correct ritual without teachers? When one acts according to [the correct] ritual, then ritual will leave one feeling at peace. When one speaks

according to what the teacher says, then one has knowledge like the teacher's. When the performance of ritual renders emotions peaceful, and when one's knowledge matches that of one's teacher, then one is a sage.

Xunzi 23.17
Any common person can become [like legendary sage-ruler] Yu.

The ideal of the princely man is relatively straightforward. Originally a political term that designated the actual heir to the throne, it represented the goal of ethical rulership enacted through ritual mastery. While ultimately unattainable, it served as a useful marker that Confucius and his students could keep in front of them to stay properly oriented. The sage (*sheng*) was a different matter. The term belonged to multiple philosophical and religious traditions and could mean several things. Even within Confucianism, its meaning could vary, and different generations of thinkers could disagree on what it signified, whether it was attainable, and which figures from the past one could consider qualified for the title. It clearly meant a person whose accomplishments far exceeded those of any princely man.

The China scholar Robert Eno describes the notion of the sage succinctly:

Early [Confucianism] shares with a number of other systems of thought the belief that an extraordinary level of understanding exists, attainable by man, which can comprehend the phenomenal world as a whole. When this level of understanding is attained, any significant phenomenon will be perceived as possessing a clear meaning because it will be understood in its relation to the whole. In other words, the multiplicity of the world makes sense, and it is possible to understand the holistic sense of it, and so to understand any part in relation to the whole.[2]

The sage possessed more than just knowledge; the sage knew the *meaning* of everything as well. A person who mastered this total intuitive vision could, based on it, always act within any given situation with consummate skill. Seeing the overall patterns of things, they could anticipate the outcome of every action without resorting to divination. They were perfect knowers and perfect actors.

They were also perfect rulers who could be distinguished from princely men by the fact that they had no teachers to show them the Way. Heaven taught them directly through its example. As the first quotation above illustrates, Confucius observed how the North Star did nothing but assume its rightful place and all the other stars revolved around it. He goes on to say in another of the quotations heading this section that the legendary emperor Yao took his cue from the natural workings of the heavens and achieved brilliant success as a ruler. Earlier we also saw that in *Analects* 15.5, Confucius praises Yao's successor Shun as one who did no more than ascend the throne and sit correctly facing south and everything in the empire worked as it should. However, in the other quotations above, it appears that Confucius did not consider the sage an attainable goal for his own followers, and in fact there was no need for such a goal. The examples of the sages of the past could serve to inspire, but since their Way had been recorded and preserved along with the examples of the early Zhou kings, no one needed to emulate them entirely. It was enough to become princely men and establish humane government in the present.

However, as the citation from Mencius shows, later generations of his followers were not convinced that present scholar-officials should not aspire to sagehood. Mencius demystifies the sage by stating that they are human just as he is human, concluding that what they achieved is not out of reach. Xunzi, in his essay on cultivating the self, laid out the course of study in three stages beginning with the "knight" or retainer (*shi*) who loves and practices the law, to the princely man (*junzi*) whose will is firm, to the "sagely person" (*shengren*) whose understanding is all-encompassing and whose thought is never exhausted (Xunzi, *Xiushen* 2.8). What happened to make the ambition to be a sage more realistic?

The intellectual environment had changed. Confucius, as we have seen, directed his teachings exclusively to young men whose ultimate ambition was to serve their government. While he certainly sought to instill in them a love of learning and an aspiration to govern with a vision of the good, he did not have to frame his ideas within a larger philosophical view of human nature. In fact, the *Analects* tells us that this was a topic upon which his students could not "hear his views" (see chapter 5). By the time of Mencius and Xunzi, however, the atmosphere had changed in two significant ways. First, the consolidation of states meant there were fewer courts seeking counselors and tutors, so when looking for such work, applicants found themselves in more competition, and it became necessary to argue for the superiority of their views. Second, as we saw in the first chapter, the establishment of the Jixia Academy in the kingdom of Qi brought thinkers together in an institution in which they earned their living by debating their ideas with rival thinkers on a more abstract level.

We will see in the next chapter that the question of human nature came forward as a topic of discussion at the academy, and both Mencius and Xunzi developed and debated theories on the matter. What is important here is that they were now thinking about human nature *as such* and pondering what could be said about *all* people, whether they aspired to government service or not. For these debates, the political term "princely man" did not serve as well, and a less political ideal became necessary. While Confucius and many others used the term to describe celestially gifted rulers from the deep past, other traditions also used the term in less politically inflected ways. Thus, in their discussions it made sense to use the word "sage" as a term that could designate the final goal of human cultivation and leave the question of fitness to govern to one side. This move entailed a trade-off, however. Sagehood came down a peg and no longer included the more mystical characteristics of the ancients. Thus, Mencius and Xunzi declared that no essential difference separated the sage from the ordinary people of their day, and with the proper drive and application, anyone could become a sage.

誠

SINCERITY

Great Learning
Things being investigated, knowledge became complete. Their knowledge being complete, their thoughts were sincere. Their thoughts being sincere, their hearts were then rectified.[3]

Doctrine of the Mean 23
It is only he who is possessed of the most complete sincerity that can exist under heaven, who can give its full development to his nature. Able to give its full development to his own nature, he can do the same to the nature of other men. Able to give its full development to the nature of other men, he can give their full development to the natures of animals and things. Able to give their full development to the natures of creatures and things, he can assist the transforming and nourishing powers of Heaven and Earth. Able to assist the transforming and

nourishing powers of Heaven and Earth, he may with Heaven and Earth form a [trinity].[4]

Doctrine of the Mean 24

Next to the above is he who cultivates to the utmost the shoots of goodness in him. From those he can attain to the possession of sincerity. This sincerity becomes apparent. From being apparent, it becomes manifest. From being manifest, it becomes brilliant. Brilliant, it affects others. Affecting others, they are changed by it. Changed by it, they are transformed. It is only he who is possessed of the most complete sincerity that can exist under heaven, who can transform.

Doctrine of the Mean 25

It is characteristic of the most entire sincerity to be able to foreknow.

Doctrine of the Mean 26

Sincerity is that whereby self-completion is affected, and its way is that by which man must direct himself. Sincerity is the end and beginning of things; without sincerity there would be nothing. On this account, the [princely man] regards the attainment of sincerity as the most excellent thing. The possessor of sincerity does not merely accomplish the self-completion of himself. With this quality he completes other men and things also. The completing himself shows his perfect virtue. The completing other men and things shows his knowledge. [. . .] Therefore, whenever he, the entirely sincere man, employs them—that is, these virtues—their action will be right. [. . .] Such being its nature, without any display, it becomes manifested; without any movement, it produces changes; and without any effort, it accomplishes its ends.

"Princely man" and "sage" were the nouns; now let us turn to the adjectives that describe the qualities that make someone exemplary. The word commonly translated as "sincerity" (*cheng*) only occurs twice in the *Analects*, and in neither case does it seem to refer to this virtue. However, two other early Confucian classics, the *Great Learning* and the *Doctrine of the Mean*, elevate the term to the status of moral ideal and discuss it at length. Confucian revivalists of later generations adopted it as such, and in modern times it has become a name for the goal of many religious traditions in East Asia. We will focus on its meanings in the early texts.

"Sincerity," as seen in the quotations above, has a number of meanings. Mencius uses it often, but only as a synonym for "truly" or "indeed." In Xunzi, it acquires more moral force, as when he says, "For the princely man to nurture his mind, nothing excels sincerity. Once he has perfected sincerity, he need have no other concern" (*Xunzi* 3.9). As seen in the quotation above, the *Great Learning* says that making thoughts sincere is one of eight steps in a program of self-cultivation. The sense here is that if we investigate things and extend our knowledge, then our thoughts and intentions become sincere. That is to say, knowing the affairs of the world and human society will enlighten us so that we can wish for the good without duplicity. In this way, it seems to correspond with Confucius's statement that by the age of seventy he could do whatever he wished because his desires no longer violated ritual propriety. His volitions had become sincere because of his long life of practical learning. In these cases, sincerity seems to indicate a kind of moral transparency, a lack of duplicitousness, and a sense that in the sincere person "what you see is what you get."

However, in the *Doctrine of the Mean*, sincerity takes on almost mystical qualities. One who achieves it becomes like the legendary sages of antiquity as seen previously. A person of absolute sincerity is minutely attuned to nature and functions as do

Heaven and Earth, covering all and supporting all without taking any overt action. He or she has foreknowledge of things to come. Like Yao and Shun, they can act as benevolent rulers simply by taking their proper position *as* rulers. According to the quotations at the head of this section, sincerity wells up from within those who have perfected it, and it shines into the world and transforms the people around them.

David Hall and Roger T. Ames have suggested that in contexts such as these, we should replace "sincerity" with "creativity" in our translations.[5] This is clear from the passage given above from the *Doctrine of the Mean* section 22, in which the absolutely sincere person participates in the creative and nourishing processes of nature. However, by "creativity" they also mean the actions of a person who combines ritual mastery with deep insight so that in applying the norms of society creatively they bring forth something genuinely new. An example from modern practice may help to clarify this.

Imagine a horn player who performs big band jazz. To fit into that setting, the player must be familiar with all the conventions of the big band: showing up for rehearsals, attending to the bandleader's instructions, cooperating with other band members, and most importantly, adhering to the canons of big band jazz as a musical genre. Without all these elements of "ritual propriety" in place, the player cannot function at all in this setting. However, they also need to infuse their performance with something extra, showing that they have the spirit of the music in hand and can use it to bring their performance to life. This will give their playing authenticity and avoid the impression of just going through the motions and slavishly following a dry formula. This fulfills the need to infuse ritual propriety with appropriateness, but let's go one step further. During each piece, the player will be called upon to stand and take a solo. This takes them beyond simply reading the music and playing with gusto. It requires that they put something of themselves into the music that, while still respecting the musical form, applies its norms in new and surprising ways. If they can do this well, it will reveal new dimensions of big band jazz and bring delight to the other players and the audience.

In these early texts, then, "sincerity" can mean a total investment in the project of co-creating the harmonious society based on extensive knowledge of ritual forms. It can mean participation in family and society in a way that goes well beyond mere adherence to convention and brings new depth to the social experience of others. Finally, it can mean mastery of the total knowledge of the ancient sages that enables them to unite with Heaven and Earth in keeping the world, encompassing both nature and human society, working together productively. In the last quotation from the *Doctrine of the Mean* above, this is equivalent to mastering "humanity," to which we now turn.

仁

HUMANITY

Analects 7.30
The Master said, "Is [humanity] a thing remote? I wish [for humanity], and lo! [humanity] is at hand."

Analects 9.29
The Master said, "The wise are free from perplexities; the [humane] from anxiety; and the bold from fear."

Analects 12.1
Yan Yuan asked about [humanity]. The Master said, "To subdue one's self and return to propriety, is [humanity]. If a man can for one day subdue himself and return to propriety, all

under heaven will ascribe [humanity] to him. Is the practice of [humanity] from a man himself, or is it from others?" Yan Yuan said, "I beg to ask the steps of that process." The Master replied, "Look not at what is contrary to [ritual] propriety; listen not to what is contrary to [ritual] propriety; speak not what is contrary to [ritual] propriety; make no movement which is contrary to [ritual] propriety." Yan Yuan then said, "Though I am deficient in intelligence and vigor, I will make it my business to practice this lesson."

I want to tell you about a character I made up called Cousin Elmo. Cousin Elmo does his own thing and does not care what other people think. When his grandmother died, he came to the funeral with untamed hair, a flannel shirt over a black T-shirt, blue jeans with holes in the knees, and grungy sneakers. During the service, he noticed several other family members looking sidelong at him and scowling. During the reception after the funeral service, several members confronted him, saying, "Could you not be bothered to clean yourself up just this once? Don't you have any respect?" Cousin Elmo grew angry and declared, "I loved Grandma just as much as the rest of you and I'm just as sorry she's gone. But I'm not going to put on some costume and pretend to be someone else for the rest of you guys. I'm going to be who I am!" While some family members accepted this, others still thought a funeral is not the time to "just be yourself." The ritual occasion demands that you dress and behave properly.

For many years I have told this story and asked my students what they thought, and in the discussion that follows I have found them to be as divided as the family members. Many agree that a funeral is a solemn enough occasion that you should adhere to the norms and not be so concerned about authenticity or individual expression. Others side with Cousin Elmo, agreeing that if the way he presents himself represents "who he really is," then there is no need to paper that over with a false display. After all, during her lifetime, Grandma herself presumably was used to seeing him wearing his usual garb and didn't mind.

The discussion on one occasion, however, demonstrated the different ways Westerners and East Asians think about the matter. I once taught a class exclusively for international students, and the class included several South Koreans whose English was just fluent enough to stay afloat. They generally did not participate much in class. However, upon hearing about Cousin Elmo, they became quite animated and broke into a long discussion among themselves about the details of proper funeral conduct. I have never encountered another group of students who were so knowledgeable about or cared so deeply for the finer points of funeral etiquette.

The primary reason students give for opposing Cousin Elmo gets to the heart of our present purpose of understanding the Confucian virtue of humanity (*ren*). Even though my students share the Western tendency toward individualism, believe that we have an inner core that constitutes our "real self," and think that our outward presentation should express this inner identity, they still acknowledge that a funeral is not about the attendees but about the deceased. They fault Cousin Elmo for taking attention away from Grandma and calling it upon himself. They also believe that in doing so, he creates divisions during an event that should bring the family closer together. Cousin Elmo's assertion of his individuality ends up frustrating one of the main purposes of the ritual.

As seen in the passage from *Analects* 17.21 quoted in a previous chapter, Confucius agrees with Cousin Elmo up to a point. In a parallel case, he speaks with his student Zai Wo about the customary three-year mourning period prescribed for elite men after the death of either parent, which involved withdrawing from their occupation, living in a mourning hut, wearing simple garments, and eating plain food. Zai Wo holds firm to his position that even a single year of mourning would be wasteful and unnecessary. Upon hearing that Zai Wo would feel fine wearing brocades and maintaining his regular diet, Confucius tells him to carry on. As we have already seen, Confucius did not condone rituals carried out mechanically and elsewhere in the *Analects* says that funeral rituals should express genuine grief. However, once Zai Wo has left, Confucius tells his other disciples that Zai Wo lacks the virtue of humanity precisely because he cannot muster up gratitude for the three years during which his parents devoted their lives to his care after he was born or generate an honest desire to repay them through the ritual.

What then is "humanity?" It is a difficult term to fix since Confucius himself was notoriously unwilling to define it or identify any specific person as embodying it. We can begin to understand the concept a little by looking at the way it is written:

$$仁 = 人 + 二$$

The first character is "humanity." As we see, it is a compound word formed by combining two other characters, the first of which means "human being" or "person," and the second of which is the number two. It is a virtue that appears only between people, not manifesting in the individual but in the interactions between people. This helps make sense of the fact that almost all other Confucian virtues have effect only when two or more people are present to each other: "trustworthiness" (*xin*), "loyalty" (*zhong*), "reciprocity" (*shu*), "dutifulness to elders" (*xiao*), and so on. We do not see some virtues found in Western culture that can apply to lone individuals, such as purity or faith. We also note that these virtues aim toward maintaining harmony and cooperation within an in-group. There are no Confucian hermits.

The example of Zai Wo also reminds us that the completion of human character requires both ritual propriety and appropriateness, and now we see that *ren* is the result of this confluence. Zai Wo might have come closer to full humanity had he both mastered the rituals of mourning and animated their performance with genuine feelings of grief and gratitude. This is not new. We have already seen this, and what we gain here is simply the name of the virtue that results from bringing ritual's form and spirit together. The story of Cousin Elmo also seems to repeat the lessons of the musician who did not want to dress appropriately to play Carnegie Hall. We might simply wish to tell Cousin Elmo to stop assuming he has an unchangeable inner core to which his outward presentation must always conform and accept that wearing a proper suit to funerals will cause his inner self to grow into the ritual in a way that feels authentic.

However, we want to go one step further to see what danger Cousin Elmo is really in. For this, we need to look at another way in which early Confucian texts defined the virtue of humanity. A statement found in the earliest Chinese dictionary and in several early classics including the *Doctrine of the Mean* reads as follows:[6]

仁, 人也

The literal meaning would be "that which is 'humanity' is the human being." In other words, to have the virtue of humanity is to be human. It does not say that "humanity" is a quality potentially achievable by human beings; it says that to have this virtue *is to be human*. What are the implications of this?

They become clearer when we remember that in early Chinese thought, nothing is identified by its being or essence but by its dynamics. We also need to bear in mind that when Confucian thinkers articulated any goal, whether it be the princely man, the sage, sincerity, or humanity, they never thought that these were perfectly achievable by any individual. They remain markers that we keep in front of us so that by orienting ourselves in their direction we may "attain the Way," and by moving ever closer to them, we approximate them more and more. So far it has seemed that human beings are the ones who attain the Way and make lifelong progress toward these goals. Now it becomes apparent that these goals define what it is to be human at all.

The difference between this notion and Western ideas about what it means to be human could not be more stark. In the West, we simply *are* human beings. Having human DNA and being biologically a human organism is enough to establish this as a fact. In Confucianism, by contrast, it appears that no one is ever fully human. Another way to put it might be to say that being biologically human is not the same as being a moral person. One becomes more human by doing what human beings do—that is, form connections with each other and set up systems of ritual norms that govern our behavior so as to knit the community together in harmony. Failing to do so constitutes a retreat from our full humanity. Cousin Elmo is doing much more than selfishly asserting himself and sowing divisions in a ritual that ought to bring family members together. He is quite literally making himself less human by doing so.

What happens when having human DNA does not establish that one is a full human being and indeed that full humanity remains forever a receding goal that no one ever reaches? What happens to our notion of human rights? I can illustrate the difference via a case study I was asked to do early in my career. The case study concerned abortion.[7]

The case involved a woman in modern China who found herself pregnant with her second child. At the time, China's "one-child policy" was still in effect, but in the case of rural families the government allowed for a second child. Her first child was a girl, and the family was hoping that she would now produce a son to carry on the patriline and maintain the sacrifices to the ancestors. Thus, when they asked her to have an ultrasound, she knew the reason: they wanted to know the baby's gender, and if it was a girl, she would be pressured to abort so they could try again for a boy. She resisted this request, feeling strongly that she did not want to "kill her child." This put her in conflict with her husband's family.

In studying the Confucian sources bearing on this issue, I found nothing that recognized either the fetus's "right to life" or the mother's "right to choose." Both claims would be based on Western notions that, first, both the mother and baby are inherently human beings and, second, on that basis enjoyed a human right that overrode any other person's concern. This runs directly counter to Western tendencies to impute full human personhood to anyone with human DNA and to focus on the individual. Instead, the sources placed an emphasis on the process by which the family worked out its differences. The decision to proceed with the ultrasound and possibly an abortion did not matter as much as whether the decision-making process strengthened the solidarity of the family or drove wedges between its members. Ritual propriety within the family hierarchy gave elders of the husband's family authority in the matter, but they were not supposed to wield it in a tyrannical way. Whether the decision was to abort or not, the most important moral issue was whether the process leading to the decision furthered each family member's progress toward humanity or led away from it.

This led to the insight that the Western pro-life and pro-choice positions, for all their strident opposition to each other, are both based in a Western framework, one in which human beings simply *are* human beings and that rights accrue to the individual. These positions are thus very close, differing only in the matter of *when* those rights take effect. The Confucian position, based in an entirely different moral framework, would find both positions incomprehensible. Both center the interest of a single individual, whether the mother or the child, in the decision-making process. Such an assertion of individual sovereignty to the exclusion of input from significant others takes one away from the goal. One becomes less human.

We have one last issue to address. All the above might make it appear that no one ever achieves the goal of *ren*, or humanity. It remains, as we have seen, a lifelong quest. Depending upon how we conduct our lives, we might move toward it for a time, but we may also backslide. However, in the first quotation from *Analects* 7.30, Confucius says humanity is never far away but is there as soon as he wishes it. How do we reconcile these two ideas? Once again, we must examine the Western assumptions that make such statements appear contradictory.

If we continue to think that we "are" human beings and that humanity is a "state," then we will have difficulty understanding the matter. Such thinking leads us to conclude that Confucius is saying that humanity is a state that is always before us but never reached but at the same time is already fully achieved the moment we want it. However, if we remember that what is important is to "attain the Way" and that it is the journey that matters, then the puzzle resolves itself quickly. In his 1972 book, Herbert Fingarette suggested that the very desire to achieve *ren* itself constitutes *ren*. One becomes human by forming the intention to face the right direction and proceed forward. As he puts it, "From this perspective it is easy to be *ren*: simply, be *ren*!"[8] Even though Fingarette himself did not avoid the use of the verb *to be*, his point is clear. One attains the Way by attaining the Way, and one may do this in the single instant it takes to form the resolution. Cousin Elmo does not have to wait until he has purchased a new wardrobe and mastered funeral protocols to achieve humanity. It will be his the minute he decides to change his ways and be a better family member. The path is the goal.

SUMMING UP

We have explored four ways in which Confucius and his followers understood the goal of human development. As the "princely man," they took a term that generally meant a man occupying a high government position and recast it as the man (and it was always a man) who had received a broad education that gave him the technical skills needed to govern, the refinement that comes from the mastery of poetry and music, and a broad and benevolent outlook that enabled him to sacrifice petty ends to serve the greater good. This was the training that drew many of his students to him, as seen by the number of times they asked him questions about good government (e.g., 12.7, 12.9, 12.14).

As "the sage," the tradition reached back into antiquity to bring forward examples of rulers who, through intense personal cultivation, brought almost supernatural abilities to the task of governing. Even contemporaries living in a less magical world could draw inspiration from their thorough benevolence and the charisma that enabled them to bring peace and prosperity to their people by the sheer power of their presence without having to enact laws or issue commands.

In certain texts, the term "sincerity" seemed to describe the moral quality that gave these ancient sages their powers of presence and all-encompassing knowledge. On a more mundane level, it could indicate a moral transparency, a "what you see is what you get" personality that evoked trust and confidence. However, it is the quality of "humanity" that stands out as the goal most prized in the tradition. An ever-receding goal that, while never achieved, kept one oriented and moving in the right direction, it both preceded the study of ritual propriety by giving it the proper motivation and came at the end once ritual propriety gave it form and appropriateness gave it spirit. It denoted the achievement of complete moral personhood, making one maximally human. It manifested in conduct that contributed to the harmonizing and strengthening of the social bonds between people.

This leads us to explore the relationship between individual moral cultivation and the enhancement of human society. Confucian training aimed at making the individual an active participant in the social project. While humanity shows itself in the bonds between people, it is still the individual's responsibility to cultivate the self so as to have a positive impact on others. The next task was to design proper methods for training, which required two steps. First, reflections on human nature sought to determine what educators had to work with so they could formulate the best teaching methods. Afterward, they could go about designing the methods themselves. Human nature and personal cultivation will be our topics for the next two chapters.

5

HUMAN NATURE
性

Analects 5.13
Zi Gong said, "The Master's personal displays of his principles and ordinary descriptions of them may be heard. His discourses about [human] nature, and the way of Heaven, cannot be heard."

Analects 17.2
The Master said, "By nature, men are nearly alike; by practice, they get to be wide apart."

Confucius had no particular interest in the question of human nature, as seen in the two passages above. These are the only two verses in the *Analects* in which the word "nature" (*xing*) even occurs. He never found himself in the position of having to argue his views at an abstract philosophical level, and his students did not need to worry about the question. He took all people to be roughly the same by nature, yet he frequently evaluated his students in various ways, and in some instances explicitly modified his teachings based on the differences between them (see

Analects 11.22). Thus, his view that human nature remains nearly constant did not lead him to adopt a "one size fits all" approach to teaching. Instead, he made it a point to gauge every student as an individual to teach them in the most effective way.

However, as we saw earlier, later generations of Confucian teachers weighed in on the philosophical question of human nature. In places such as the Jixia Academy in the state of Qi, they came face to face with rival thinkers who demanded a more systematic presentation in lecture and debate. A variety of views emerged from both Confucians and teachers of other schools: human nature was entirely good, it was entirely evil, it was unfixed and became good or evil in response to upbringing, it varied such that some people were good and others evil, and so on. For Confucians, the question became important because human nature dictated teaching methods. If humans were wholly good by nature, then one style of moral education would be most suitable, while if their nature was evil, then they needed a different approach. In this chapter, we will review the famous dichotomy between the later thinkers Mencius and Xunzi. The former held that human nature was entirely good, while the latter thought it was completely evil.

Before exploring their views, however, we need to understand what these thinkers meant by "human nature," because it differs greatly from the Western definition. In the West, let us remind ourselves, we see human beings as having an essence; we *are* something. Historically, questions about human nature sought to define what we are at our core, as distinct from "accidents," features such as blond hair or variations in intelligence, that were simply overlays that did not affect our basic substance. Again, while not all Westerners are philosophers, we do tend to take "human nature" as referring to this unchanging substance. We are Popeye the Sailor declaring, "I yam what I yam!"

In early China, however, the view was dynamic, and "human nature" referred not to an underlying substance but to a tendency, a direction, developmental patterns, behaviors. We can open the discussion by once again examining some Chinese characters, this time arranged in the logical sequence "A is to B as C is to D."

生 : 成 :: 性 : 誠

The first character can mean "birth," "production," and "life," based on its depiction of a sprouting plant that has just broken ground. The second character broadly means "completion" or "maturity." Thus, they indicate the beginning and end of a process of growth. If you look at the second pair of characters closely, you will notice that the first two form the right half of each of them respectively. The third character is the "nature" of "human nature," and the fourth is "sincerity," a concept we have already explored. The relationship that I want to draw attention to is that between human nature and sincerity. Human nature stands for the beginning of the process, while sincerity is the hoped-for end.

This should make clear that in Confucian texts, to say that human nature is good, evil, both, or variable is to identify its initial trajectory. If, as Mencius asserted, human nature is wholly good, then its most natural course of development will be toward virtue, and the most appropriate educational style will be one that nurtures it along and keeps it on track. On the other hand, if human nature is completely evil, as Xunzi declared, then moral education will first need to radically redirect it and cause it to develop in a way that he said would be artificial and not natural.

Now that we understand that in Confucianism "human nature" refers to a natural direction of development and not an enduring essence, let us see how Mencius and Xunzi each argued their cases. Doing so will reveal new insights about both Confucianism and Western culture.

MENCIUS: HUMAN NATURE IS WHOLLY GOOD

Mencius 6A.2

Master Gao said, "Human nature is like swiftly running water. If a breach is made in the east, it will flow eastward. If a breach is made in the west, it will flow westward. Human nature is indifferent to good and evil the same way that water is indifferent to east and west." Mencius said, "Water is indifferent to east and west, but is it indifferent to up and down? The goodness of human nature is like water flowing downward. There is nothing in human nature that does not tend toward goodness just as there is nothing in water that does not flow downward. Now you may slap water with your hand and make it go over your forehead. You can also conduct water up a mountain. Are these really in accordance with the nature of water? [No,] they come about when one applies force [to it]. You can force people away from goodness, but with regard to human nature [itself], the case is the same."

Mencius 6A.7

Mencius said, "When the harvest is abundant, the younger generation will mostly act virtuously. When the harvest is scant, they will mostly turn to violence. The difference does not originate with the capacities Heaven bestows on them. It comes about because they submerge their [naturally good] minds."

Mencius 6A.10

Therefore, there are things that I want [such as virtue] more than life, and things that I detest [such as wrongdoing] more than death. It is not just the worthies who have this mind. All people possess it, it is just that the worthies are able to avoid losing it. If one can get a small basket of rice and a simple platter of soup, one can live. Not getting them, one will die. Still if they are offered with insults, no passerby will accept them; if stepped on, not even a beggar will take them.

Mencius developed his theory that human nature is entirely good based on the idea of the Four Sprouts (*si duan*). These were four innate tendencies found even in small children, and while they did not constitute mature moral virtues in themselves, they were the seedlings from which the virtues would grow. When a child falls in the playground and scrapes his knee, other children will come around and try to comfort him. This is commiseration, which can be grown into humanity (*ren*). Any child can feel shame when caught with her hand in the cookie jar, and this sense of shame can grow into righteousness (*yi*),[1] or fully mature morality. They instinctively feel respect for parents and teachers, and when properly cultivated, this feeling turns into ritual propriety (*li*). Finally, all children approve of some things and disapprove of others, and this inclination to choose can grow into wisdom (*zhi*). Mencius asserts that none of these are infused from outside; all are inherent in the nature of children, and the fact that this natural endowment provides the basis for developing virtue means that their nature is inherently good.[2]

However, we can still ask if the presence of the Four Sprouts of virtue prove that human nature is *wholly* good. Mencius spent a lot of time debating with another thinker named Gaozi, or Master Gao, who thought that human nature did not have a fixed direction for development and could be led toward either good or evil, as seen in the first selection above. For Master Gao, anything inborn counted as human nature, including the needs for food and sex. Assuming these needs exist alongside the Four Sprouts, should we not at least say that human nature is a mix of opposing tendencies? Mencius's response to this was to deny that inclinations toward food, sex, or other animal needs formed part of human nature; human nature comprised *only* the Four Sprouts. This should raise a red flag. If human nature consists of the Four Sprouts and does not include any other tendency, and if the Four Sprouts lead toward virtue, then essentially Mencius has already won the debate. If only the good comprises human nature, then of course human nature will be wholly good. As I learned in my high school speech class, the person who controls the definitions wins the debate.

However, something deeper is at play here, and to understand it, we need to remember once more that in the process-oriented world of early Chinese thought, we are always striving to become more human; humanity is not a feature that belongs to every biologically human organism regardless of moral development. Humanity is a directional marker, and we are either progressing toward it or moving away from it with every action and every moral choice. In this light, we can see the question that Mencius is really raising: What makes us human? Master Gao is not wrong in saying that the need for food and sex are inborn, but according to Mencius, these cannot be developed into traits that make us more human. Quite the opposite. Sometimes they impede the development of humanity, and the demands of self-cultivation might even override such basic needs as food and survival. As shown in the quotation above, people will refuse food if offered in a way that demeans them. In other places, Mencius says that moral people will face dangers and court death in pursuit of the right. Thus, Mencius is not so much defining the term "human nature" in such a way as to guarantee he wins the debate as stating that it is only as we develop the good that we become increasingly human. The Four Sprouts, as the incipient tendencies that lead toward virtue, are also the beginnings of humanity itself.

There was another obvious objection to Mencius's view. One may look around and see truly evil people in the world, some so terrible that it is hard to believe they ever had a nature that initially pointed them toward virtue. How can one maintain the innate goodness of human nature in the face of such counter-examples as Adolf Hitler or Pol Pot? Mencius himself did not worry too much about this. After all, the Four Sprouts were simply the beginning impulses that set people moving toward the good. As with actual plants, going from incipient sprouts to full moral virtues required care and cultivation, and if the sprouts did not receive these, they would not mature. This is why in passages such as that from 6A.10 above, Mencius says that what separates most people from the "worthies" (*xian*, a word akin to "sage") is not that they lack these innate sprouts of virtue but that they lost them along the way, while the worthies were able to preserve them. This being so, Mencius fully expected to see evil people in the world around him.

How might one lose the sprouts? One way was through inept child-rearing and poor education. This might include abuse and neglect, but it could also include the well-intentioned application of educational methods not suited to human nature. To illustrate this, Mencius told the story of a farmer from the state of Song who wanted his rice to grow faster, so he went into his field, grabbed each stalk, and pulled it upward. In the end he succeeded only in uprooting all his plants and destroying his crop (*Mencius* 2A.2). His intention was right, but his method was wrong. In the same way, the use of inappropriate educational methods, even by well-meaning parents and teachers, can throw moral development off its natural course.

After we grow up, then, we become responsible for keeping ourselves on track in the journey toward full humanity. To demonstrate how deeply rooted the Four Sprouts are, Mencius told another parable about a traveler on the road who looks to one side and sees a child about to fall into a well (*Mencius* 2A.6). Any person will instantly feel alarmed and start rushing over to save the child. No other thought will intervene, whether for reward or reputation. The feeling is immediate and strong. Mencius concluded by saying this shows that one of the Four Sprouts, commiseration, naturally abides within each human being. However, he did not say that everyone will act on that feeling; he only affirmed that it would arise. If the traveler has second thoughts about being late for something or of not wanting to get involved, then they might well suppress the feeling and go on their way. The innately good sprout was present, but because the traveler did not act on it, its growth was stunted, and for this they are wholly responsible. It is only by letting our nature follow its own course of development that we become the equals of the ancient sages and worthies.

Mencius brings all this together in his parable of Ox Mountain (*Mencius* 6A.8):

Mencius said, "Ox Mountain once had beautiful trees. Because it sat next to a great state, [men] chopped at them with axes and hatchets, so could we [still] consider them beautiful? With the rest it got in the day and the night, and the moistening it received from the dew, there was no lack of new shoots sprouting up. But then cattle and sheep were put to pasture on it, and so it became bald as it is now. People, seeing how bald it is, believe it never had any timber, but can that really be the nature of the mountain? Can the human mind really be lacking in humanity (*ren*) and righteousness (*yi*)? When they lose their innately good minds, is it not like the axes and hatchets coming day after day to chop the trees? Could we still consider them beautiful? After resting during the day and night and inhaling the clear *qi* of the morning, their likes and dislikes come back a little to being like those of other people, but the things they do during the day reverse the effect. When this happens time after time, then even the night air is not enough to preserve them, and when the night air is no longer sufficient to preserve them, then their behavior is not far from that of wild birds and beasts. People see that they are like wild animals and think that they must never have had the basic potential to be human. But is that what they were originally like? Thus, there is nothing that will not grow if given proper care and nourishment, and nothing that will not wither if deprived of these."

The mountain represents the person so evil that people do not believe they ever had any potential for good. Mencius points out that by nature, this mountain should be teeming with plant life. Its current bald state arises from interference of two kinds, each of which represents a possible way that human nature may be thrown off course. First, people came and clear-cut the mountain, which is like a child suffering under abuse, neglect, or unsuitable teaching. In her book *For Your Own Good*, the psychologist Alice Miller describes the child-rearing practices by which Adolf Hitler was raised, and we may well wonder how history might have played out if he had been nurtured differently. But childhood experience is not the end of the story, which leads to the second point.

After all the trees have been cut down, seeds and roots remain in the ground and vegetation will soon start to grow back. In the same way, even someone whose development was stymied in childhood might still grow up to be a moral adult. However, if livestock grazes on the mountain and nips off all the new growth, the day will come when everything is eradicated, leaving no chance for renewal. This is like a person whose continual wrongdoing prevents their nature from ever developing as it should. When the traveler suppresses the impulse to save the child from falling into the well, it is as if an animal had nipped off the sprout of commiseration and kept it from growing and strengthening. Once the sprouts are gone and the growth of virtue becomes impossible, then, as Mencius says here and in other places, one is no longer human; the person has become an animal.

In sum, when Mencius declares that human nature is completely good, he is referring to the normal course of human development, not a fixed moral quality possessed even by a baby in its bassinet. As a seed or sprout, it still requires care and nurture to reach its full potential. At first parents and teachers provide this care, but later in life the person becomes responsible for continuing their growth toward full human personhood. As we have seen before, they never fully reach this goal, but as long as they have "attained the Way" and make steady progress toward it, that is all we can ask. If we see evil people around us, it is not because they lacked this from the beginning (try to picture an evil baby) but because external factors interfered with the seedlings and even uprooted them completely. As long as we remember that "human nature" in early China refers to dynamic patterns of development and behavior, this makes sense. This implies that moral education will work best when it accords with the natural trajectory of human development, helps it along, and does not interfere with it. In the next chapter we will see how Mencius lays out the way that education works with human nature, but for now let us turn to an opposing view.

XUNZI: HUMAN NATURE IS WHOLLY EVIL

Xunzi 23.1
Human nature is evil. Virtue comes about [only] artificially.

Xunzi 23.4
In general, "inborn nature" is what comes spontaneously from Heaven. It does not involve either study or application.

Xunzi 23.10
As a rule, people want to become virtuous [precisely] because their inborn nature is evil.

A generation later, the Confucian thinker Xunzi declared his complete disagreement with Mencius and proposed that human nature is completely evil. Mapping out his position will enable us to see with greater clarity the scope of ritual propriety within Confucian thought and give us new insights into our own society.

When we say Mencius believed human nature to be wholly good and Xunzi believed it to be wholly evil, we imply that their positions are utterly contradictory. However, once we dig into the details, we see that the two thinkers were actually talking past each other for two reasons. First, they defined "human nature" in different ways, meaning that they were not talking about exactly the same thing. Second, they used different approaches to argue their points. As we have just seen, Mencius argued from individual psychology: the Four Sprouts were tendencies within the individual mind, and he focused his discussion on how they developed. Xunzi argued from sociological and economic behavior, asking what would happen on a large scale if human nature took its natural course.

When Mencius said that the Four Sprouts defined human nature, he excluded other innate tendencies because they lead us away from full humanity if we let them run loose. As seen in the second quotation above, Xunzi did not exclude these things from his understanding of human nature. For him, human nature consisted of whatever tendencies occur naturally in people. Thus, in section 23.2 of his book, he declares that love of profit, envy, hatred, and sensual desires are part of human nature, and when people follow these inborn inclinations, then all manner of social evils ensue. While Mencius would say that such behaviors come from letting go of our natural tendency toward virtue, Xunzi says that they come precisely from following our nature. Thus, although the subject under discussion is "human nature," it turns out that the two men are not talking about the same thing, and so naturally they arrive at different judgments.

Xunzi shows what he means by saying,

> According to their inborn nature, people want to eat when hungry, seek warmth when cold, and desire rest after labor. These are their natural inclinations. However, when they see their elders, they will not dare to eat first but will defer to them. Even when tired, they will not dare to take their rest, but will take over their elders' work to relieve them. These two practices—that is, the son deferring to his father or the younger brother deferring to the older, and the son taking over his father's work or the younger brother relieving the older's chores—violate inborn nature and are contrary to natural inclinations. Nevertheless, they constitute the way of filial piety and the refined rationality of ritual propriety and benevolence. Therefore, following natural inclinations and inborn nature leads to violations of the proper order of deference, while the proper order of deference runs afoul of natural inclinations and inborn nature. Taking all this into consideration, it is clear that human nature is evil and that virtue comes from unnatural effort. (23.6)

In other words, what is inborn and does not need to be learned is to eat when hungry and rest when tired. Proper training in the

Way, however, teaches us not to follow these natural impulses. This preserves proper order and harmonizes relationships within our social groups by inculcating habits of self-denial that do not accord with human nature.

Second, while Mencius argued from the standpoint of individual developmental psychology (the Four Sprouts and their growth), Xunzi argued from a sociological and economic perspective. For a junior member of the family to hang back and refrain from eating until the elders have finished is not just an act of courtesy; it is also a way of distributing food so that everyone can be sure they will get what they need. In section 23.7, he gives another example of how ritual propriety shapes economic life. Here he describes two brothers who come into a store of valuable goods. Their inborn nature, which includes a love of profit, will lead them to quarrel and fight over the goods if not checked by the ritual deference of younger to older. Following the rules of propriety acquired through training that override their natural inclinations, they will achieve an equitable distribution with which both can be content. On a larger scale, Xunzi asks his readers to consider what would happen if all the rules of ritual propriety and morality were to disappear along with all the structures of hierarchy and authority put in place by the ancient sage-kings. If Mencius is correct, people would cope with the sudden anarchy by cooperating and helping one another. He thinks the real outcome would be chaos and the law of the jungle (*Xunzi* 23.9).

From his position that human nature is wholly good, Mencius had to account for the existence of truly evil people, as we have already seen. Xunzi had the opposite objection to answer: If human nature is inherently evil, then why is there any goodness at all in the world? Why does the situation just described not prevail in all times and places? Xunzi responds that, paradoxically, it is precisely because human nature is evil that the norms of ritual propriety and morality appear. People may be evil, but they are also rational and can see that giving free rein to their amoral tendencies will lead to misery for all. This is the point of the third quotation at the head of this section: the human desire to do good springs from the realization that our nature is evil and thus in need of external control.

On observing that in Xunzi's reading ritual propriety goes beyond mere etiquette and veers into economic regulation, I began to wonder if there were any analogues in our own society. Are there instances where social conventions rather than market forces dictate how goods and services flow? I found one humorous example while looking at a church supply catalog many years ago. This was a high-end catalog issued by an Italian firm, and the first item featured was a set of papal robes. A man in his fifties modeled the garments, and the catalog gave no price for the set. I remember wondering what was the point of advertising such a product when the target demographic consists of only one person in the world? In connection with Xunzi, I further reflected that there must be a lot of people who could afford to buy these robes, and if they chose not to, the reason was that they were not entitled to wear them. Ritual propriety dictated who had the right to appear in them. We can easily think of other instances of this kind. I sometimes ask my students if they have ever thought of buying a police uniform. The fact that they laugh at the thought shows that they have deeply absorbed the prohibition on wearing the uniform when they are not members of the force. It is not that they can't afford it. It just isn't done, that's all.

I found a more encompassing example when I thought back to my childhood growing up in a military family. For most of my childhood, we lived in military housing on various Air Force bases, and I saw regular interactions between members of the armed forces. One could certainly detect a system of deference expressed through ritual gestures: every member of the military knows who they salute and who salutes them, who stands at attention when who enters the room, and who speaks freely to whom and who calls whom "sir." Ritual propriety also dictates the symbols worn on the uniform.

More than this, however, the system also allocated goods, services, and resources. One's rank determined one's pay grade to be sure, but it also determined where one lived. I remember housing located on the side of a gentle upward incline. The base commander's house was the single detached home with the largest yard. As you proceeded down the slope, you passed the houses of the colonels, majors, captains, and lieutenants, with the bachelor officers' quarters below the rest. Then there was The Street that divided officers' housing from enlisted personnel housing. At the far end were the barracks for the newly recruited airmen.[3] There was an Officers' Club where commissioned officers went with their families to swim in the pool, eat in the cafeteria, and drink at the bar. The noncommissioned officers had their own club. Xunzi would have understood all of this very well.

While this may seem to go against some Western ideals, those who make a career of military service generally appreciate the clarity of relationships in this system and are happy to abide within it. While the military may be the most thoroughgoing example of Xunzi's ideas about ritual propriety in Western culture, we can find other instances without much difficulty. As noted before, my own experience as a university professor relating to colleagues and students shows some of the same features.

Reading Xunzi gives the impression that for him, ritual propriety is unnatural and artificial, the very opposite of authentic. I would agree with this only to a limited extent. Xunzi certainly states over and over again that human nature, left to itself, leads to reckless and selfish behavior; that is why he considers it evil.

However, as we shall see later, there were other thinkers who agreed with his assessment and thought that people need external controls (human police or divine supervision) to suppress their tendencies to antisocial behavior. Xunzi remains a Confucian because he believes that ritual propriety and morality can be instilled in people to such a degree that it becomes second nature, and thus people can be made to regulate themselves without external coercion.

Think of the example of a handshake once more. If you could travel back in time and watch your parents and teachers show you how to shake hands, you might realize that it is a learned behavior that does not come naturally and that you may even have to suppress selfish impulses to carry it off. ("I don't *want* to shake hands with him!") However, if you look at your use of the ritual gesture now, you might not see it as unnatural at all. That was Xunzi's point: while ritual propriety and morality may not come naturally, and while at the outset moral training may involve uprooting some natural behaviors, in time we can become so habituated to ritual and morality that it takes root and feels completely natural and authentic.

All this may create the appearance that Xunzi was quite sour on human life, believing as he did that human beings are by nature evil and need to be trained to suppress their impulses to make room for better habits. However, he has one more thing to say to us that balances his pessimism. In an essay on music, Xunzi declared that human beings are given to joy, need joy, and will always seek outlets for finding joy. Music, as part of ritual propriety, provides this outlet.[4] More broadly, Xunzi believed that if everyone could be trained in ritual propriety and all became sages, then life would be joyful. When everyone knows what to do in their interactions, then human social life becomes like a great dance in which everyone knows the steps and they glide around one another creating something more beautiful than any of them could have created alone. If it did not fulfill this human need for beauty, then Confucianism would serve no worthwhile purpose.

CONCLUSION: HUMAN NATURE AND HUMAN FULFILLMENT

It seems Mencius and Xunzi staked out opposing and extreme positions on human nature, the first claiming it is entirely good and the other declaring that it is 100 percent evil. It should now be clear that they were not engaged in a direct confrontation. Xunzi came later, and so Mencius could never have addressed his objections, and when we read Xunzi's critique of Mencius, it seems he did not quite get what Mencius had said. In the end, both are solid Confucians because both believe that through education and self-cultivation, anyone can become like the sage-kings of antiquity. Both opposed reliance on coercion, whether through human enforcement or divine retribution, to maintain order. External control only motivated people to obey to the least extent necessary to stay out of trouble and always caused them to look for loopholes and evasions. Self-cultivation in ritual propriety, a broad humanistic education, and immersion in the arts made people self-regulating, considerate, and added beauty to their lives. Their only real difference was in the means of education they thought best suited human nature. Did it consist of cultivating the sprouts of virtue already present to maximize their growth, or was it to suppress what was naturally there and replace it with virtues that could be inculcated deeply enough to feel natural? If the first, then a Waldorf School education would work best. If the latter, then something more like a military academy is indicated.

The main purpose of this chapter has not been to evaluate their arguments and decide which of them, if either, was correct.

Modern psychology shows that both positions are untenable. The real value of this examination has been to see another way of framing the question of human nature as a dynamic process that leads either toward or away from a moral personhood that is never fully accomplished. It has also shown that even in Western culture, some Confucian ideas operate in a way that Western individualism and substantialism hide from us. If our study does not demonstrate this, learning how they thought about the matter would be a mere academic exercise with no relevance to us. I hope to have shown that this dive into their ways of thinking has shed light both on ancient Chinese thought and the world we live in today.

6

PERSONAL CULTIVATION
修身

Analects 1.4
The philosopher Zeng said, "I daily examine myself on three points: whether, in transacting business for others, I may have been not faithful; whether, in intercourse with friends, I may have been not sincere; whether I may have not mastered and practiced the instructions of my teacher."

Analects 12.24
The philosopher Zeng said, "The [princely man] on grounds of culture meets with his friends, and by friendship helps his [humanity]."

Xunzi 23.17
Now, if an average person could be induced to engage in study, focus his will, and ponder deeply day after day without respite, then he could penetrate through to divinity and participate in [the work of] Heaven and Earth. Therefore, a sage is [just an ordinary] person who arrived through the accumulation of long effort.

Confucian self-cultivation is a deliberate communal act. (Tu Weiming)[1]

Cultivation in the Confucian tradition takes place both in solitude and in public, the one alternating with the other. Unlike some other Asian religious traditions, Confucians do not envision solitude as a permanent state (again, there are no Confucian hermits). On the other hand, various Confucian authors have also affirmed that effective practice requires some time alone so that those on the Way may engage in focused study and self-examination. The goal, however, is always to return to the public square refreshed and ready to contribute to the common life of family, society, and nation. This careful balance of private practice and public performance mirrors the paradox of the social self. Individuals learn the norms of their society, then their ongoing participation simultaneously transmits and reshapes those norms going forward, as seen above in the discussion of the *dao* as a human Way. The Chinese characters at the head of this chapter literally mean "cultivating the body" and point to the individual side of this paradox, but all authors agree that we cannot possibly know that our self-cultivation has succeeded until we have deployed its fruits in our social interactions and gauged their effectiveness.

Here once again the analogy with language may help us understand the situation better. A person living completely apart from other human beings has no need for language; language is a social institution for communication. We do not invent language but learn it from those who have gone before us. In our conversations with other members of our language community, we inculcate it in those who follow us and help shape its development. Yet language subsists nowhere but in individual minds, and there is a sense in which we all have to take responsibility for mastering it, a task some will accomplish better than others. In the same way, the rules of ritual propriety (which we nowadays may understand as culture) operate in the same way. How did the classic Confucian authors understand this process of training and mastery?

As we look at methods of self-cultivation across several texts, we shall see that there is no consensus on a single path toward the goal of maximal humanity. Instead, we shall find several proposed paths.

TAKING THINGS IN ORDER

Let us revisit the eight-step "order of operations" for training the self laid out in the classic text the *Great Learning*:

1. Investigation of things
2. Extension of knowledge
3. Making the will sincere
4. Rectification of the mind
5. Cultivation of one's personal life
6. Regulation of the family
7. Putting the state in order
8. Bringing peace to the world[2]

The goal of this program is to "manifest the clear character, love the people, and abide in the highest good." The order of operations follows from discerning what is basic and what is derivative, or as the text puts it, distinguishing the "roots" (*ben*) from the "branches" (*mo*). Thus, cultivation of our own persons constitutes the beginning point and forms a kind of trunk from which moral actions will emerge like branches and touch the lives of those who surround us.

ben	*mo*
本	末
root	branch

This list points ahead to many of the features of Confucian self-cultivation that we will touch on in this chapter. The first five steps have to do with the individual, and they begin with education and learning. The third and fourth steps make clear that the purpose of education is not just the accumulation of facts but to direct the growth of the individual in "making the will sincere" and "rectifying the mind." In step 5, the student brings the realizations gained by this process to the conduct of affairs. Modern Chinese encapsulates all these steps in the saying "study to put into practice" (*xue yi zhi yong*). The last three steps show how the fruits of self-cultivation play out in the expanding circles of the family, the country, and finally the world. However, while this may seem to prescribe a clear movement from purely individual endeavors to social participation, in fact the student carries out even the first five steps in the company of others. Again, all practice is social practice. This follows from the fact that the "self" in Confucian thought never indicates an individual as we conceive the term today but a node in a network of relationships.[3] The "self" that requires education is always relational, so all steps from the investigation of things to the cultivation of the self take place in everyone's matrix of relationships.

學

EDUCATION

Analects 8.8

The Master said, "It is by the Odes that the mind is aroused. It is by [ritual propriety] that the character is established. It is from Music that the finish is received."

Analects 13.5
The Master said, "Though a man may be able to recite the three hundred odes, yet if, when intrusted with a governmental charge, he knows not how to act, or if, when sent to any quarter on a mission, he cannot give his replies unassisted, notwithstanding the extent of his learning, of what practical use is it?"

Like all religious or political traditions, Confucianism needed institutions to carry it from one generation to the next and to set its tone in practical affairs. From about 142 B.C.E. to 1905 C.E. (with some interruptions), Confucianism was carried forward via systems of education and a set of civil examinations, and in both the primary object was the memorization of classical texts. In school, students memorized them; in the examination hall, they demonstrated their mastery of them. When most Westerners hear about a curriculum that consists mainly of rote memorization and regurgitation, they react negatively: How is this true education? When we look at the details, however, a more complicated picture emerges.

Let us begin with the word "study" or "learning," pronounced *xue* and written with the character at the head of this section. In both ancient and modern Chinese, its meaning differs somewhat from the two English words just given. When college students in the West take a course, they are expected to master course material, and we typically measure the degree to which they have done so by testing. They may hone their skills in critical thinking via discussion and writing assignments, but in today's universities, the emphasis is on setting measurable course goals and objectives. "Character formation" is not amenable to objective measurement, and so students may come and go through our classes personally unchanged and still be considered successful. (In recent years I have mounted a small protest against the "culture of assessment" by listing "Grow in wisdom" as one of the stated goals of my courses. Assess that if you can!)

The meaning of the word *xue*, in contrast, always has a practical component in addition to denoting the simple amassing of knowledge and skill. Once, in a Buddhist temple in Taiwan, I saw a poster in the guest lobby that read "Study the Buddha" (*xue fo*). Both because of the setting and for simple grammatical reasons, the word *xue* could not reflect the meaning of the English word "study." Instead, it meant to study so as to emulate the Buddha and achieve a real transformation in your life. Thus, the meaning of *xue* is more like the ancient Greek word *phrónēsis*, which indicated practical wisdom, prudence in judgment, and excellence of character. We see this in the two quotations above about the *Book of Odes*, a set of three hundred poems that Confucius had his students memorize. He believed that having these carefully selected poems in mind helped to shape his students' character, and being able to quote from them effectively while on a diplomatic mission showed that they had the practical intelligence needed to use them constructively in consequential interactions.

For this to happen, the learner needed good teachers; there was no question here of the individual achieving illumination on his or her own. One's teachers were not necessarily the professionals who held positions in Confucian academies or private family schools. They could also be family members, friends, and informal mentors. During later periods in Chinese history, it became common for mothers to be their children's first teacher, imparting basic literacy to them so that they would be ready for formal instruction later. Under this system, girls received education along with their brothers to prepare them for this role, and materials appeared on the market such as the *Three-Character Classic* (*San zi jing*), a work that ingeniously presented three new characters per line in ascending levels of written complexity and appealing rhymes. In addition, there are many examples throughout history of a boy receiving significant portions of his formal education from his father, an uncle, an elder brother, or other relatives.

The family was the crucible for education in two other ways. It provided a child's first experience of living in a hierarchical social group. This required the child to develop awareness of the positions of all family members and the obligations and expectations appropriate to them. As Confucius's student commented, someone who had mastered filial piety as a child was unlikely to foment trouble as an adult moving in society. In addition, the family was the most natural place to learn how to express these relationships in a caring way, bringing appropriateness and ritual propriety together. Mencius in particular put forth this view in his opposition to Mozi, another thinker who proposed that expressions of caring should be universal and equal among all people (see chapter 7). Mencius noted that if someone on the road were to encounter a random corpse in a ditch, they may pass by without too much concern. However, if they discarded the body of a deceased parent in the woods, then later, upon seeing wild animals eating it and its decomposed state, they would break out in a cold sweat and return with spades and baskets to give it a proper burial (*Mencius* 3A.5). It is natural for people to feel this way about close family members and not about strangers, so the Mohist position of universal care did not accord with nature. Nevertheless, having learned to feel and express care within the family, a person could later extend it to the country and the world as they took on wider responsibilities. It is for all these reasons that the program of the *Great Learning* places regulation of family life before governing the state and bringing peace to the world. The family is the incubator of virtue.

Once the student began formal schooling, his primary activity consisted of memorizing and discussing the meaning of classic texts. *Jing*, the word for "classic," originally meant the warp threads on a weaving loom. The idea was that just as the warp threads cannot be changed once they are loaded onto the beam and the weft threads have to move around them, so these texts formed the basic framework around which other lessons and applications would need to arrange themselves. While the Confucian curriculum was said to involve other studies such as music and archery, throughout history the classics took center stage and the examination system focused on them. This meant that a lot of thought went into the selection of texts to memorize and the framework for their interpretation. As Tu Weiming put it, the ideal result is a person who is "aesthetically refined, morally excellent, and religiously profound."[4]

To begin with the selection of texts, Confucius set his own students to work on the "Six Classics" (*Liu jing*): *Book of Odes* (*Shi jing*), *Book of History* (*Shu jing*), *Record of Rites* (*Li ji*), *Book of Changes* (*Yi jing*), *Book of Music* (*Yue jing*), and *Spring and Autumn Annals* (*Chunqiu*).[5] Again, remembering that Confucius saw his mission as training young men to assume posts in government, these texts taken together formed the basis of a broad humanistic curriculum. The students who memorized and internalized the meaning of these texts would know historical precedents both ancient (*Book of History*) and recent (*Spring and Autumn Annals*), would be culturally refined (*Book of Odes* and *Book of Music*), would know the protocols of the court (*Record of Rites*), and would be able to perceive the patterns of change and gauge the potential results of various actions and policies (*Book of Changes*, to which Confucius himself reportedly contributed several commentaries). Their formal studies, coupled with the lessons learned in the family, would not only equip them to exercise wisdom and prudence in state affairs but also enable them to extend the concern they naturally felt for family members to all the citizens of the state and make peace in All-Under-Heaven (*tianxia*). In sum, they would have completed the eight-step training program that fitted them for public service.

The attainment of a position in government, however, did not hang solely upon the successful completion of this curriculum. Someone—the emperor or a local ruler—had to hire you, and this required the creation of procedures and criteria. For many centuries, rulers either created state hierarchies by ennobling allied families and giving them permanent fiefs, appointing friends and cronies to top positions, or giving posts to the highest bidder. However, even at an early date they saw some advantage to giving applicants with demonstrated qualifications a chance to serve. The result was the civil examination system, said to have begun in 142 B.C.E., when Emperor Wu of the Han dynasty personally quizzed some young men and found places for them in his administration. By the time the system was discarded in 1905, it had evolved from a simple interview with the ruler to a multilevel program of education and competitive testing that had a million men in its grasp at a time. Tourists in Nanjing today are still amazed at the last remaining wing of the examination compound, which had to seat several thousand examinees every three years.

Such a system, in which your career and the social elevation of your family depended on a single test, was bound to stir up controversy, and the terms of the disputes will be familiar to anyone in the West who has followed the fortunes of similar examinations, such as the Scholastic Aptitude Test (SAT) or Graduate Record Examination (GRE). Beyond the first part of the exam, which tested how well the candidates had memorized the classics, there were sections that required examinees to compose original essays. Disagreements centered around (1) whether the examinations were needed at all, (2) what classic texts pupils should memorize, and (3) what kind of essay would best predict a young man's suitability for office. The historian Benjamin A. Elman's *A Cultural History of Civil Examinations in Late Imperial China* provides a fine overview of all these disputes. Let us begin with the required reading list and the method of reading.

Before memorization can begin, one must know what to memorize. Afterward, one needs to know what to do after the task of memorization has been completed. As we have seen already, for Confucius the curriculum was carefully chosen to produce the "princely man," the refined, broad-minded, and intelligent individual suited for the work of teaching, administration, and diplomacy. The texts nourished these qualities, and memorization served several purposes. As Confucius himself noted about the *Book of Odes*, its contents refined students' sensibilities and enabled them to hold their own in sophisticated conversation; quotations skillfully deployed in diplomatic exchanges helped them make points and carry out responsibilities. They needed to memorize them because there was no publishing industry, and they could not count on having copies of the texts on hand. In the midst of a policy debate in court, they had to have everything at their fingertips.

The situation was very different in the Song dynasty (960–1279). By that time, a viable publishing industry had emerged and the examinations, which did not exist in Confucius's time, were extremely competitive. Many voices called for either abolition or reform of the system, none more far-reaching in its effects than that of Zhu Xi (1130–1200). He changed the reading list and formulated recommendations on study methods that he believed would yield the greatest benefit. He proposed new ideas about why to read, what to read, how to read, and when to stop reading.

Why read? Zhu Xi declared that "learning is for the self alone" (*wei ji zhi xue*). This may seem odd, given that the declared purpose of Confucian education is to enable learners to fit within and contribute to their social groups. What Zhu Xi meant to emphasize, however, was that reading and education could meet these goals best if the student undertook them for self-cultivation, not for social mobility, to impress others, to gain wealth, or for any other selfish reason. Education for these purposes would be "learning for the sake of others" (*wei ren zhi xue*). In line with the eight-step program of the *Great Learning*, we begin with the self, and from that beginning point our cultivated self can expand into the spheres of family, state, and world. If we began with the ambition to gain power, wealth, or prestige, then we would move too quickly into public life to the benefit of no one.

His answer to the second question regarding what to read had long-lasting consequences for the examination system itself. The five classics edited by Confucius were very long, written in what for Zhu Xi's time was a very difficult antiquated style, and often contained material that did not contribute to the advancement of the student's personal development. He recommended an alternative set of required books that he felt laid out the most fundamental and important concepts in a relatively easy-to-read form. These became the "Four Books": the *Analects* of Confucius, the book of *Mencius*, the *Great Learning*, and the *Doctrine of the Mean*. In an age when printing presses were inundating the reading public with many choices, he thought it better to select a limited number of excellent books, arrange them in a curriculum, and tackle them in order. Long after his death, these four works did indeed become the reading list for the examination hall.

He had recommendations on the "how" of reading as well. For the best result, he said, the student should read deeply and repeatedly. To put these recommendations into practice, he suggested that learners prepare themselves with a period of "quiet sitting" (*jing zuo*) to settle the mind and rid it of distractions. They should then read slowly, being sure to take in the ideas. He said, "You must frequently take the words of the sages and worthies and pass them before your eyes, roll them around in your mouth, and turn them over in your mind."[6] This would allow the wisdom of the ancient sages to sink in, not only as ideas to be learned but as an influence that would help mold character.

However, eventually the student had to face the world, so there came a time to put the books down. After all, what the sages of the past had recorded in the Four Books was meant to be put into operation in the ordering of family and society. Seeing how they worked in real situations would bring their ideas to life and demonstrate their value. More than that, it would reveal "principle" (*li*), the basic patterns not only of human sociality but of all things in the world. The character looks like this:

理

The word originally indicated the patterns seen inside a piece of jade. In later philosophical works it came to mean the hidden "patterns" of the world according to which events unfolded. Reading the Four Books introduced the student to the principles of things, and setting the books down and putting their lessons into action revealed their relevance to real situations. One whose education had proceeded to the point that they could function effectively to maximize the harmony of people with one another and the world around them was truly a sage.

In bringing this section on education to a conclusion, I will point out the contrast I see between the Confucian vision of education and modern Western attitudes. While in our modern culture we certainly value education and promote it as the path to self-improvement and career success, we also harbor a very deep suspicion of it. We make heroes of individuals who dropped out of the educational system and found success. We denigrate "mere book learning" and romanticize intuition, as in the *Star Wars* films when Luke Skywalker's training involves no textual study at all, and he is counseled to "reach out with your feelings." Cultural items such as Pink Floyd's song "Another Brick in the Wall" paint education as mere indoctrination meant to stifle individual creativity and flatten out personalities. We constantly struggle to understand the value of a humanistic education that does not provide a set of skills that one can immediately apply in the workplace. How many times do we hear about English majors ending up waiting tables, as if that is all they will do for the rest of their lives?

The Confucian vision has it that the wisdom of the past can still speak to us through books that broaden our vision and keep us from reinventing the wheel time and time again. Its intent was to form character and produce citizens who could go beyond their own interests or even the interests of their family to put the state in order and bring peace to the world. As someone who has spent my professional career in education, I do not think this is unrealistic.

A MODEL OF THE MORAL MIND

Analects 6.21

The Master said, "To those whose talents are above mediocrity, the highest subjects may be announced. To those who are below mediocrity, the highest subjects may not be announced."

Analects 12.21

For a morning's anger to disregard one's own life, and involve that of his parents—is not this a case of delusion?

Doctrine of the Mean 1

While there are no stirrings of pleasure, anger, sorrow, or joy, the mind may be said to be in the state of Equilibrium. When those feelings have been stirred, and they act in their due degree, there ensues what may be called the state of Harmony. This Equilibrium is the great root from which grow all the human actings in the world, and this Harmony is the universal path which they all should pursue. Let the states of equilibrium and harmony exist in perfection, and a happy order will prevail throughout heaven and earth, and all things will be nourished and flourish.

While granting that character formation and education are group enterprises, the Confucian tradition has always affirmed that it is the individual who receives, cultivates, and employs them in daily life. It also recognized that not all individuals were equal in their capacity to absorb and apply their lessons. Confucius often assessed his students' strengths and weaknesses, and, as seen in the quotation from *Analects* 6.21 above, he also directed different levels of education to students of different degrees of talent.

Mencius also acknowledged the differences in his students and in those seeking government appointments, even as he put forward his theory about the universal goodness of human nature. There was a disconnect between his and Xunzi's sweeping theories of human nature and the evident fact of individual variations, because to say human nature is entirely good or entirely evil is to make a systematic claim about all people. It fell to later Confucian thinkers to look at the psychology of the individual mind to see why some people take to education and can enact their lessons in moral life better than others.

In the Song dynasty, Confucian thinkers began to draw upon the quotation from the *Doctrine of the Mean* given above for a way to understand the moral mind and see how it could be used to predict the appropriateness of proposed actions. This text described the mind as existing in a state of balance prior to its encounter with things and situations that might arouse the emotions. If moral actors could regulate emotions through the exercise of their judgment, then the result would be harmony and all things would flourish. We should notice two things here. First, the text does not call for the elimination of emotions. It only calls for them to reach their "due degree." Emotions have always played a role in Confucian ideals of sociality, as witnessed by texts calling for affection and deep love when appropriate within a relationship. Problems ensue when emotions get out of control and bring about violations of ritual propriety. Second, if "harmony" results from successful regulation of emotion, then it must be true that its opposite results from unrestrained emotional outbursts. They called this "disorder" (*luan*). The text also makes clear that these results will be seen in not only society but also the natural world. This need not imply a mystical connection between human action and the natural order, since coordinated human action must work with nature for success in such things as agriculture, forestry, and animal husbandry.

When later thinkers expressed these ideas more systematically, something like the following diagram emerged:

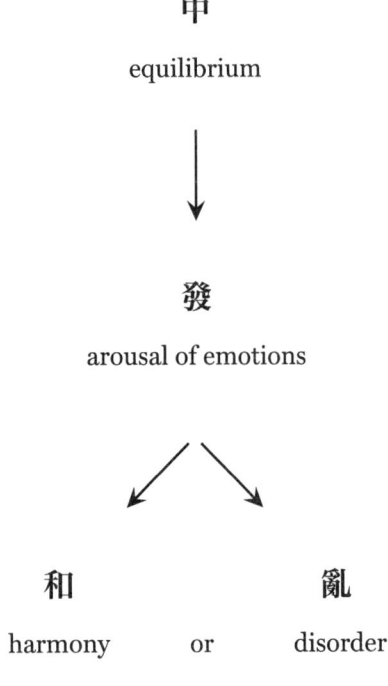

中

equilibrium

發

arousal of emotions

和   or   亂

harmony   disorder

This model portrays a mind that is originally in equilibrium prior to the stirring up of emotions in response to its encounter with external persons or situations. After such an encounter, the emotions are aroused, and the mind can go in one of two directions. Either the person controls the emotions so that they are expressed in a way suitable to the situation, resulting in harmony, or the person allows their emotions to get the better of their education and judgment, resulting in disorder. This left open two questions: First, how did education work to school the emotions? Second, why were some people better at this than others?

For Zhu Xi, whose recommendations on reading we have already seen, the answer to the first question lay in the eight-step program of the *Great Learning*. It began with the "investigation of things" and the "extension of knowledge." Reading the words of the ancient sages in the classics and putting their moral lessons to work in actual situations gave you a base of knowledge that made the next steps—gaining sincerity of the will, rectifying the mind, and personal cultivation—easier. Education gave you the clear vision to see what worked best in the world, and you could then sincerely want what was best. Rectification of the mind and personal cultivation flowed smoothly from this sincerity. However, this did not resolve the second question about differences in aptitude among individuals. To address this issue, Zhu Xi modified Mencius's theory of the inherent goodness of human nature by bringing in the concept of *qi*.

氣

The word *qi* in East Asian languages has many meanings, and readers who have studied forms of practice such as martial arts, meditation, Chinese medicine, or tai chi may understand it as a kind of breath or energy. However, in Zhu Xi's writings it refers to a primal substance out of which all matter and energy arise through self-differentiation. Some *qi* is yang in quality, making it very clear, light, warm, and active; other times, *qi* manifests in a yin form, making it turbid, heavy, cold, and passive. The makeup of all human beings combines these two basic qualities, but in some, the mix is cloudier and more turbid than in others. In other words, some people are made of more active and pliable raw material than others. Thus, when Zhu Xi said that Mencius was right in assessing human nature as wholly good, he meant that the basic plan that patterned the appearance of human beings was good. He called this plan "principle," a word we examined above.

How did the quality of someone's mix of *qi* impact their aptitude for education and capacity for moral action? Let us imagine that we have a blueprint showing us how to build a house. The blueprint was expertly drawn up; if we follow it exactly, we should have an exquisite house. However, a blueprint is not a house. To build the house, we must acquire the materials. If we get high-quality materials for the construction, then the result will be in accordance with the architect's vision. However, if we get warped lumber, damp wallboard, rusty pipes, and so on, then the house will not be good. In the same way, Zhu Xi taught that human nature is indeed aimed entirely at the growth of virtue, but if the person is made of faulty qi, then their capacity for education and cultivation will be hampered and their training will take more effort. This analogy allowed Zhu Xi to account for individual differences. One whose qi was light and clear could investigate things and extend knowledge quickly and apply the lessons in daily life almost effortlessly. For someone whose qi was of a lower grade, education would be more laborious and would involve clarifying their own qi through exposure to the classics and the influence of their teachers.

The approach of investigating the principle of one thing after another may seem piecemeal, but Zhu Xi believed that the final result would be seamlessly wholistic. Beginning with the classic texts would give us a head start, since the words of the ancient sages keep us from having to reinvent everything from scratch. Away from their desks, learners encountered both things and situations in daily life, providing them occasions to extend their knowledge by applying their lessons and assessing the results. It is important to keep in mind here that in the Confucian tradition, people do not seek knowledge for its own sake. Instead, finding the principle of things always means mastering their dynamics and seeing how things go, and this knowledge helps us determine the appropriate action to take in the future. As one of Zhu Xi's predecessors put it, knowing the principle of horses and oxen means knowing which one to hitch to a chariot and which to a cart. This is no different from knowing the principle of family dynamics and responding with the appropriate display of filial piety.

After carrying on this process of investigating things and extending knowledge throughout your life, the principles of all things and all moral situations would interlink more and more until, in an almost Zen-like epiphany, they fused together and you perceived the Principle (the capital P is intentional) of all things as a unity. Ideally, you would then be a sage. As a sage, you would be a stranger to nothing and could act in such a way as to produce and maintain harmony with human society and the natural world at all times. While it might be more difficult for those born with turbid qi, the efforts made in attaining such knowledge would remove the obscurations and strain out the impurities. As right knowledge and action improved the quality of your qi, the inherently good nature that Mencius said constituted the basic "blueprint" for all people would manifest more and more distinctly, just as removing the defective parts of a house and replacing them with higher-quality materials would reveal the excellence of the architect's design. Thus, everyone could in theory achieve sagehood no matter the quality of their initial endowment of qi.

Zhu Xi's approach was objective. Training involved studying texts using his reading tips and test-driving what you learned in actual situations. You would know whether you had acted properly or not by observing the results. If your actions resulted in social harmony, then you would know the action was correct. If you saw disorder, then you would know that the action was inappropriate, and you could undertake the necessary steps to correct course. As we saw in the case of the family pressuring their daughter-in-law to get an ultrasound, the tradition judged their action not by Western standards of right and wrong but by whether the process they followed to resolve the matter left the family unit in harmony or conflict.

In the Ming dynasty (1368–1644), another Confucian thinker arose and reconfigured this process along more subjective lines. Wang Yangming (1472–1529) spent significant time practicing Zen meditation and studying Daoist philosophy. When he heard about Zhu Xi's method of studying the principles of things one by one, he was intrigued and decided to try it for himself. Thus, in 1492, he and a friend positioned themselves by a stand of bamboo and gazed at it, hoping to intuit the principle of bamboo. Wang's friend gave up after three days, and four days later Wang himself caught a cold and had to go home with nothing to show for his effort. At that point, he decided Zhu Xi's approach did not live up to its promise and tried a different tack. Rather than looking outward to find objective principles in the external world, he would look inward to the nature of the mind itself. Building on Mencius's idea that human nature already possesses the seeds of virtue, Wang concluded that the mind already contained knowledge of the good even when at rest. However, when encountering things in the world, the activated mind could become clouded by selfish desires, obscuring its innate goodness and throwing it off-balance. The key to right action, therefore, was to examine the mind at rest to grasp its innate moral principles and then take a moment before acting to compare one's proposed action with the moral mind. For Wang, the question of whether your qi was clear or cloudy was irrelevant.

If we look once more at the diagram above through the lens of Wang's teachings, then the course of an action would look like this: The mind at equilibrium already knows what is right, but when it is aroused by the emotions, it can lose its bearings, causing us to act recklessly. If we first stop and think about the impulse to act in a moment of emotional arousal, then we can see whether it accords with our innate virtue. If so, then the mind will return to equilibrium directly after the action is done, leaving us at ease. Otherwise, the mind will be flustered and out of balance. In order to carry out Wang's guidelines, we need a way to examine the mind at equilibrium to familiarize ourselves with its in-built morality. For this, Wang recommended a form of meditation derived from the Zen practice of observing one's own mind to detect its innate buddha-nature. He determined that this process of introspection was what the phrase "the investigation of things" meant, and that the "extension of knowledge" did not mean the accumulation of objective facts but taking what we innately knew and extending it into the world through our actions.

However, when his students put his recommendations into practice, the results were not quite what he had envisioned. Rather than using the technique to establish a baseline against which to gauge the morality of their prospective actions, several of them grew enamored of meditation itself and did not move on to the next step of using it to help them in daily life. In fact, after Wang's death, many of the Chinese literati developed a keen interest in Zen, and one commentator stated that Wang Yangming's teaching had provided the opening for the subsequent "Buddhist revival" of the late Ming dynasty. As a remedy, Wang rethought the notion of the mind at equilibrium. The mind was never really at rest, but it could be in balance nevertheless, and instead of engaging in periods of formal seated meditation, his disciples could use the technique of introspection to monitor the mind right in the midst of daily life.

To help us understand this, think of two ways that things can be in balance. One would be a static balance, as when the two pans of a scale come to rest if the weights in both of them are equal. The other could be a dynamic balance, as when two trained dancers join hands and turn around a common center. It is the equalizing of their opposing forces that keeps the dance together, and when it works, it is beautiful. Thus, the mind at equilibrium did not have to be blank or still. We can go about our daily business with the mind in equipoise, and upon encountering a situation that arouses our emotions, we can react in a way that keeps the mind moving in harmony or in a way that throws it off-balance. The action that preserves the balance of the inherently moral mind and maintains its calm will be the correct choice.

Zhu Xi took "principle" to mean the moral patterns discoverable through observation of both nature and human social behavior, while for Wang Yangming it meant moral principles present in the mind from the very beginning. This meant that for Zhu Xi, moral education entailed studying the classics, observing the external world closely, discerning its patterns, and acting in such a way that one's behavior preserved harmony in both the natural world and one's social group. For Wang it meant studying the classic texts to pick up clues about the nature of the mind, then engaging in introspection to see the moral principle already there directly. Since aroused emotions could blur these innate moral instincts, one had to observe the mind in equilibrium so that one could know when it was being clouded. Then one could uncover it and bring it to bear on whatever situation had stimulated the emotional response and act correctly. Zhu Xi's approach came to be called the "School of Principle" (*li xue*), while Wang's took the name "School of the Mind" (*xin xue*).

In my opinion, both men make valid points. When we go about our daily lives, we find ourselves navigating many situations that require us to exercise judgment and seek the best way forward. We generally look both outward and inward to assess the situation and examine our own values. After acting, we look to see whether our response has helped settle the situation or created further disturbance, and whether our minds are at ease with our choices or flustered and in disarray. At the end of the day (literally), we can examine ourselves to see what we can learn from our successes and failures both objectively and subjectively.

SOME CONCLUDING THOUGHTS

The questions raised in this chapter crop up in ongoing Western debates about education just as much as they did in imperial China, and despite the distance between the two in time, geography, and culture, the terms of the debates can strike us as familiar. Should there be a uniform curriculum for all? If so, what should we include in it? Is there any value in standardized examinations? If so, what should they test? What should our educational system prepare students for? How do students learn? Should formal education help students form character? If so, how?

The differences between the approaches of Zhu Xi and Wang Yangming also echo some of our own culture's perplexities about learning. A certain strain of thought in the West sees the merit of an outwardly aimed education. Learning about the external world and our fellow citizens has definite value. There are also those who, like Wang Yangming, think that everything we need is already built into us, and all we need to do is look within to make enlightened choices. It can seem like a debate between the "head" and the "heart," between book learning and trusting our gut instincts. Depending upon how we judge the correctness of our actions, Zhu Xi's recommendation that we look at the level of harmony or disorder that our behavior causes in the world around us may look like seeking approval from others, while Wang's style of seeing whether the mind remains in balance or is flustered after our actions might look like not letting others dictate our behaviors and attitudes.

Except for those at the outer ends of the bell curve, I wonder how many people actually make that choice and stick to it consistently. I will conclude by noting that this mind versus heart dichotomy never really arose in China because a single Chinese character stands for both the mind and the heart:

心

Perhaps most of us intuit that the two form a unity and the kind of education that prepares us best for life in our world will keep the two connected and working harmoniously together.

7

DISSENTERS

Analects 13.11
The Master said, "'If good men were to govern a country in succession for a hundred years, they would be able to transform the violently bad, and dispense with capital punishments.' True indeed is this saying!"

Analects 14.38
Zi Lu happening to pass the night in Shi Men (Stone Gate), the gatekeeper said to him, "Whom do you come from?" Zi Lu said, "From [Confucius's household]." "It is he, is it not?" said the other, "who knows the impracticable nature of the times and yet will be doing in them."

Confucianism holds out the prospect that through education and practical application, people can become entirely self-regulating. As the ruler governs through ritual propriety, virtue will radiate out through his ministers to the people and the performance of the rites will lend beauty to the citizens' lives. Since the people will have an innate sense of right and wrong and be trained to express it through the rites, laws and punishments will be unnecessary; and if a ruler must resort to them, then that ruler has failed.

Not surprisingly, many thinkers contemporary with Confucius and his first generations of followers thought such a vision unrealistic or undesirable. We will look at three dissents from the Warring States period (475–221 B.C.E.). The first two, put forth by the Legalists and the Mohists, argued that some kind of external coercion is needed to maintain order because we cannot count on the population to police its own behavior. The third, mounted by the Daoists, held that there was more to the good life than just playing one's role in society and that ritual propriety, far from enhancing our humanity, was stultifying in its effect. For them, following the Way of the larger natural world presented a more rewarding alternative.[1]

法家
THE LEGALIST CHALLENGE

Hanfeizi 50
Now Yao and Shun cannot come to life again. Who is going to determine the truth of Confucianism or Mohism? . . . To be sure of anything without corroborating evidence is stupidity, and to base one's argument on anything about which one cannot be sure is perjury. . . . Such learning, characterized by stupidity and perjury and such an unrefined and conflicting [doctrine] practiced [by the Confucianists and Mohists] are unacceptable to an enlightened ruler.[2]

Hanfeizi 49
[T]here are many in the world whose talks are devoted to argumentation and who are not thorough when it comes to practical utility. That is why even when the hall of the ruler is

full of scholars who praise ancient kings and preach humanity and righteousness, the government is still not free from disorder.[3]

Hanfeizi 49
Confucius was a sage known throughout the empire. He cultivated his own character and elucidated his doctrines and traveled extensively within the four seas. People within the four seas loved his doctrine of humanity and praised his doctrine of righteousness. And yet only seventy people became his devoted pupils.[4]

The Legalist school was known for its pragmatism, adaptability, and a drive toward power that veered toward authoritarianism. While Machiavelli-style advice had been set down in writing before, a school taking the name "Legalism" (*fajia*) did not appear until the third century B.C.E. Its most prominent founding figures were, interestingly, students of Xunzi. They accepted Xunzi's notion that human nature was intrinsically evil but did not share his faith that human beings were amenable to reform through ritual or any kind of morality radiating from the emperor outward. The most prominent of these founders was Hanfeizi, or Master Hanfei (before 281–233 B.C.E.).

As seen in the first quotation above, Hanfeizi put no stock in the teachings of the ancient sage rulers. As he pointed out, they lived thousands of years in the past, so no one could be entirely sure what they had actually said or done. For proof, he pointed out that the Confucians and the Mohists had very different ideas about what these legendary rulers practiced and the lessons we should draw from them. In any case, their times were different. They ruled over a much simpler society in a time of relative peace, while Hanfeizi's own era, the Warring States period, was far more complex and chaotic. This period required attention to the actual situation at hand and the development of appropriate responses, not slavish devotion to ancient and irrelevant ideals. As he makes clear in the second quotation above and throughout his works, what matters is concrete accomplishment, not airy talk about "humanity" and "righteousness."

Believing that human beings for the most part were incapable of moral self-regulation, he championed the need for the ruler to hold the means of power—rewards and punishments—in his own hands. If he were to rely on the appearance of naturally good people for the success of his state, then he might as well search high and low for a naturally straight piece of wood to make an arrow or a naturally circular slab to make wheels. The army needs many arrows *now*, so arrowsmiths must straighten crooked wood forcefully to meet the need, and people need a lot of wheels *now*, so wheelwrights must steam and bend wood to produce them.[5] Noting that, despite the wide appeal of his teachings, Confucius only attracted seventy pupils, Hanfeizi asserts that the state simply cannot hope that a Confucian educational system will reliably produce a critical mass of humane and righteous citizens. People need laws to follow and an assurance that rewards will accrue to those who submit and punishment be exacted from those who disobey.

We can feel the force of Hanfeizi's argument. Indeed, it might have occurred to you that the Confucian project seems rather utopian. Could any society implement such an effective and universal program of moral training that it could dispense entirely with police, courts, laws, and prisons? As I have thought about this issue over the years, I have also wondered about the workability of Hanfeizi's scheme. Can state power alone maintain social order? Running a totalitarian state requires a lot of resources and manpower: not just police but spies and secret police, suppression of dissent, monitoring of the press, and so on. It seems to me that any state, if it is to run efficiently and with the goodwill of its people, must hope that most of its citizens will be moral and self-controlled. Confucius and his followers were correct to think that, without some interiorized intuition of right and wrong, and without some sense that those in power share this sense and govern in accordance with it, then most people will simply become evasive and calculating, and life would not be good for anyone. In the final analysis, Confucius and Hanfeizi both have valid points, and a system that includes moral education combined with a code of enforceable laws works best.

墨子
THE MOHIST ALTERNATIVE

Mozi 15.2

Nowadays lords of estates know only to love their own fiefs, but not those of others; so they do not hesitate to promote their own and attack others. Nowadays heads of families know only to love their own households, but not those of others; so they do not hesitate to promote their own and pillage others. Nowadays individuals know only to love themselves but not others, so they do not hesitate to promote themselves and rob others. . . . All the disasters, pillaging, anger, and hatred in the world arise from the lack of mutual love, and thus people of humanity decry them.

Mozi 26.5

So I say that for each murder of an innocent person one calamity will follow. Who is it that murders the innocent? Human beings. Who is it that inflicts calamity? Heaven. . . . This is how I know that Heaven loves all the common people of the world.

Mozi 25.4

If the doctrines of those who advocate elaborate funerals and extended mourning are followed . . . mourners would weep in a confused manner to the point of choking, wear sackcloth on the breast and flax on the head, keep the snivel dangling, live in a mourning hut, sleep on straw, and rest their heads on a lump of earth . . . all this is to last for three years. . . . So, much wealth is buried in elaborate funerals and long periods of work are suspended in extended mourning. Wealth that is already produced is carried to be buried and wealth yet to be produced is long delayed. To seek wealth in this way is like seeking a harvest by stopping farming.

The philosopher Mozi (480?–400? B.C.E.) and his movement are not well known among Westerners now, but in the centuries after Confucius's death, Mohism was a major contender on the political scene. Like Confucius, Master Mo deplored the constant instability and warfare of the Warring States period and sought to establish teachings to bring peace and security. Interestingly, he was a military engineer, and part of his effort involved assisting cities in designing defensive structures that would be formidable enough to discourage others from laying siege. His movement is noted for promoting the idea of universal love (*jian ai*), its belief in a Heaven that actively watches human behavior and responds with rewards and punishments, its utilitarianism, its empirical methods of investigation, and its opposition to rituals. Here we will look only at universal love, Heaven, and ritual.

As seen in the first quotation, Mozi thought that many of the evils of the world would end if only people loved each other universally without distinction. In saying this, he was directly contradicting the Confucian idea that society fell into different groups such as families, fiefdoms, and states, all of which had internal responsibilities. To be clear, however, Mozi did not teach individuals that they should cultivate this feeling of love within themselves. Instead, he wanted it implemented as a governmental policy, and showed from historical examples that if the emperor makes it known that he wants his ministers and subjects to act in certain ways, the people will obey. Mencius, as we have seen, pushed back against Mozi's idea by arguing that universal love was not natural.

We saw this when we noted how Mencius said a person could encounter a random corpse by the side of the road and not be too bothered by the sight, but if it were the corpse of their parent, then they would be very upset and see to its proper burial. This tendency could subsequently be developed into a more universal concern as they took on wider responsibilities locally, regionally, and nationally. Indeed, there are examples of Confucian officials throughout history who implemented programs to collect abandoned bodies and give them proper burials. This point is also borne out by the eight-step program of the *Doctrine of the Mean*, in which people extend the fruits of their cultivation from the self to the family to the nation. Confucians consistently argued that Mozi's recommendation, being against the natural growth of human morality, would be ineffective. It was like the farmer from Song pulling up his rice plants in an effort to make them grow faster.

Mozi, like the Legalists, also did not believe that enough human beings in society could achieve self-regulation to ensure the security of all. They needed rewards and punishments to induce good behavior. However, unlike the Legalists, he saw Heaven as the agent that would enforce morality, not the ruler. In his view, Heaven was conscious and monitored human behavior, assigning rewards and inflicting punishments as appropriate. In response to both Mozi and the Legalists, later Confucians asserted that doing what was right without regard for personal consequences showed a higher level of moral development than any system of rewards and punishments could produce. From Confucius onward, the tradition claimed that if the coercive force of carrots and sticks offered the only incentive for good behavior, then people would simply become calculating. There is a saying in Chinese that seems to repudiate both the Mohist and Legalist positions: "Heaven is high and the emperor is far away" (*tian gao di yuan*), meaning that no one is watching, and people can do as they please. Confucians believed that training in ritual propriety would create citizens who understood and respected morality, and their behavior would reflect a personal investment in good relations rather than a calculation of benefit and harm.

Mozi was a utilitarian who had no patience for ritual propriety as a way of smoothing human relations and eliciting the cooperation of Heaven. The third quotation above is taken from his essay against elaborate funerals, which he saw as a waste of precious resources. He describes all the effort that goes into constructing an imperial tomb and lists the massive amounts of grave goods that are buried with the monarch, and he observes that all that work and all those goods could have been used for more concrete benefits such as feeding and clothing people. In a separate essay, he pours contempt on the troupes of musicians and dancers employed at the royal court. They do not spin or sew, yet they wear fine costumes. They do not sow or reap, but they still eat. They are mere parasites.

It was to this that Xunzi replied when he said that rituals such as elaborate funerals and fine music adorn life with beauty, which he saw as a need equal to the material needs for food, clothing, and shelter. As to the time wasted when a capable official retired for three years (in practice, twenty-five months) following the death of either parent, Confucius himself had defended this custom as a means of repaying the kindness of parents who had spent the first three years of their child's life focused on their protection and care. Mozi, as a utilitarian, did not value these things. For him, whatever did not directly address the material needs of all the people was a waste of time and resources. The Confucians held that life should consist of more than bare subsistence activities. Ritual propriety not only elicited Heaven's cooperation in the production of material necessities but rendered life worth living. This is a topic about which people disagree to this day.

莊子
A DAOIST CRITIQUE: ZHUANGZI

Zhuangzi 17

Zhuangzi was once fishing beside the Pu River when two emissaries brought him a message from the king of Chu: "The king would like to trouble you with the control of all his realm." Zhuangzi, holding fast to his fishing pole, without so much as turning his head, said, "I have heard there is a sacred turtle in Chu, already dead for three thousand years, which the king keeps in a bamboo chest high in his shrine. Do you think this turtle would prefer to be dead and having his carcass exalted or alive and dragging his backside through the mud?" The emissaries said, "Alive and dragging his backside through the mud." Zhuangzi said, "Get out of here! I too will drag my backside through the mud!"[6]

Zhuangzi 22

Ritual Propriety is just a mutual swindling. . . . Hence, it is said, "When the [Way] is lost, there is [Virtue]; when [Virtue] is lost, there is Humanity; when Humanity is lost, there is Ritual Propriety. Ritual Propriety is the fruitless flower of the [Way] and the beginning of disaster."[7]

Zhuangzi 13

Duke Huan, seated above in his hall, was (once) reading a book, and the wheelwright Bian was making a wheel below it. Laying aside his hammer and chisel, Bian went up the steps, and said, "I venture to ask your Grace what words you are reading?" The duke said, "The words of the sages." "Are those sages alive?" Bian continued. "They are dead," was the reply. "Then," said the other, "what you, my Ruler, are reading are only the dregs and sediments of those old men." The duke said, "How should you, a wheelwright, have anything to say about the book which I am reading? If you can explain yourself, very well; if you cannot, you shall die!" The wheelwright said, "Your servant will look at the thing from the point of view of his own art. In making a wheel, if I proceed gently, that is pleasant enough, but the workmanship is not strong; if I proceed violently, that is toilsome and the joinings do not fit. If the movements of my hand are neither (too) gentle nor (too) violent, the idea in my mind is realized. But I cannot tell (how to do this) by word of mouth; there is a knack in it. I cannot teach the knack to my son, nor can my son learn it from me. Thus it is that I am in my seventieth year, and am (still) making wheels in my old age. But these ancients, and what it was not possible for them to convey, are dead and gone: so then what you, my Ruler, are reading is but their dregs and sediments!"[8]

The book of *Zhuangzi*, a Daoist text from the Warring States period, is relentless in its criticism of Confucius and his teachings. Zhuangzi's critique is complex and profound, so here I will focus on a couple of points as illustrated by the quotations above.

The first quotation shows Zhuangzi fishing in a river when some messengers arrive from the court of Chu, the largest state in this period. They present him with the king of Chu's invitation to serve as his prime minister, an invitation that any of Confucius's disciples would have been elated to receive. Zhuangzi, however, turns it down brusquely, and the story he tells to justify his refusal reveals much about his disagreement with the Confucian project. To understand this, we need to ask why Zhuangzi brings up a sacred turtle.

As Zhuangzi explains it, the king of Chu has the body of a turtle that has been dead for three thousand years in the shrine of his ancestors. We know from archaeological finds that turtle shells were used in divination, and these shells were indeed preserved for long periods of time. The fact that this turtle is kept in a shrine in which the king regularly performs rituals to honor his ancestors implies that the king and his ministers use the turtle as a ritual implement. Zhuangzi next asks whether this is what the turtle would have wanted or whether it would rather be alive in its natural environment, and the emissaries are forced to admit that it would likely rather be alive and following its own path than be dead and used in human rituals. Zhuangzi then sends them on their way, declaring that he, too, would rather pursue his own natural inclinations.

As we saw earlier, life in a royal court at any time was bound up with a host of rituals. Part of the promise of Confucian teaching was that adherence to ritual propriety made you more refined and broad-minded, and in the last resort, more *human*. This is the point Zhuangzi disputes with his analogy. As a prime minister, he would be bound by all the most minute details of court ritual, and he claims that far from fulfilling his humanity, it would actually crush it under the weight of artificial protocols just as surely as being made into a ritual object killed the turtle. Thus, this first quotation shows a very sharp divide between the two men over what makes us human. Confucius, Mencius, and Xunzi all said that mastery of ritual (both courtly and quotidian) would complete us as human beings by enabling us to interact harmoniously with others. We could participate in rituals as if in a great dance. Zhuangzi believes that following our inborn nature is the key to expressing our humanity. To go to bed when sleepy, eat when hungry, and sit by the river fishing if he takes a notion are much more authentic ways to be human than entanglement in the oppressive constraints of ritual propriety.

Confucians might dismiss this as pure selfishness, but the second quotation shows that there is more to Zhuangzi's dissent than a simple wish to follow his own natural rhythms. Like the other great Daoist classic, the *Daodejing*, Zhuangzi romanticizes the rustic life of far simpler societies. In small villages of illiterate country folk, the division of labor was much less complex, society was not stratified into classes, and everyone could know everyone else. In this setting, he believes, no one needs to learn the virtues or even to name them; it all came spontaneously. The fact that Confucians (and others) have to come along later and identify virtues and train people to follow them only indicates how much of this primordial simplicity has been lost. Zhuangzi, living in a cabin and fishing in the river, mounts a living protest against the complexities of society and a demonstration that a return to simplicity is possible.

Finally, the third quotation attacks the Confucian educational program. As we have seen, Confucius took great care to prepare a set of core texts for his students to memorize and discuss in the belief that doing so would not only fit them with the knowledge needed to function within the government but also refine them and point out the Way. Zhuangzi, on the other hand, regards the ability to live a good life as a matter of skill rather than knowledge and refinement. As the wheelwright says, you cannot learn how to carve a wheel simply by reading a how-to book; you have to set your hand to the task and *do* it. You might make many mistakes along the way, but in the end, it is practice, not study, that will instill the knack. Likewise, what the duke is reading—no doubt a Confucian classic—is only the "dregs and sediments" of the ancients and will not help him to govern. He needs to put the book down and get on with governing.[9]

Zhuangzi had much more to say about the Confucian path, but this will do for our purposes. We will conclude this chapter by seeing how the Confucians responded to these challenges.

BRINGING CONFUCIUS INTO REAL LIFE

Confucianism easily overcame the challenges of Legalism and Mohism; the Daoist critique had a deeper impact and prompted adjustments to its implementation.

The Legalists and Mohists both cast doubt on the Confucian proposal that everyone in the state could be made self-governing by instilling ritual propriety in them. They could not foresee any future in which everyone watched over their own behavior to the extent that there was no need for external controls in the form of vigorous law enforcement or a punishing deity. However, rulers, while agreeing with this sentiment insofar as no Chinese emperor ever attempted eliminating all means of control, still saw the danger of going too far in the direction of these two rival schools and depending solely on external force. The result would be a police state in which every citizen needed to be watched, and even the watchers would need to be watched. Such a police state is extremely resource-intensive and impractical, and so by officially adopting Confucianism as state orthodoxy, they hoped that the maximum possible number of citizens would indeed watch over themselves and minimize the need for law enforcement. It is the same in our own society. While we understand that we cannot do away with the highway patrol, we still plan on most drivers watching their own behavior on the road so that we will not have to deploy an overly large number of officers just to keep the roads safe.

At a deeper level, Confucians frequently observed that when social morality depends upon external rules and enforcement, everyone from the ruler on down becomes an amateur lawyer and begins looking for loopholes, exceptions, and special circumstances. Amid all this calculation, the spirit of the law yields to its letter. As Mencius put it, everyone begins to look for ways to game the system to their own advantage. In contrast, a personal commitment to the Way keeps people constantly aware of the ultimate purpose of social morality: human happiness and a flourishing community. Furthermore, Confucian teachers and authors noted that regulating one's behavior solely to gain rewards and avoid penalties was not as good as following a personal commitment to cultivating humanity. Rewards and punishments lead individuals to do only the minimum required to profit themselves and avoid loss, while a personal quest to achieve humanity leads them to maximize their efforts to grow in righteousness.

The movement known as neo-Confucianism attempted to meet the Daoist and Buddhist alternatives in various ways. Here is one example: Zhu Xi, the Song-dynasty figure whose recommendations on reading we examined above, saw the point of Zhuangzi's critique of reading classics as the means to attain the Way. However, whereas Zhuangzi seems to want to abolish reading altogether in favor of direct engagement with the activities of life, Zhu Xi contextualized the Confucian reading program as but one component of a good life, not the whole of it. According to him, reading the classics gives you a head start. By seeing what the sages of old had to say about the Way, you do not have to rediscover the Way from scratch; you can pick up clues that will help move you along more rapidly. Zhu Xi said that, in the end, we must put the books down and throw ourselves into the messy project of living day to day. We may not be able to carve a wheel successfully simply by reading a book on the subject, but if we read a book or even receive some oral instruction on it, we might make fewer mistakes at the outset and get the knack sooner.

As to following our own nature instead of channeling our behavior into the ritual protocols that attach to various social roles (or "dragging one's backside in the mud" instead of being a dead ritual implement), the social history of Confucianism shows that many of the literati already accepted this criticism to some extent. While they might well insist on performing their duties conscientiously, they often resisted being nothing more than mere roles within society, family, or government. Many of them studied Daoist and Buddhist philosophy or undertook practices in their spare time, as if to acknowledge that there was something to them that was not reducible to a set of roles, and they undertook regular retreats or meditative practices to recover their own inner selves before returning to work and family.

In the West, we tend to see "religions" as mutually exclusive options: if you commit to one, then you do not practice or believe the others. However, even today most Chinese see religions as resources from which they may select for various life needs. Thus, with few exceptions, a person's commitment to the Confucian Way did not preclude delving into Daoism or Buddhism if they offered something that might help them through a situation or resolve a perplexity. During my travels in Taiwan and China, people would often complain to me that Western religions were too exclusive, and census data often show that the sum of the percentages of people who say they practice various religions is more than one hundred. Seen in this light, the arguments of the dissenters are not so much anti-Confucian as they are ways to point out the limitations of a strictly exclusionary commitment to Confucianism. Confucian writing often did the same for these other traditions. The result was a religious ecosystem in which all participants kept each other in balance.

8

HOW DID CONFUCIUS CHANGE MY MIND?

While I hope that by now you have learned a thing or two about Confucianism, this book is not a textbook on the tradition. A textbook would have to be much thicker and introduce a lot more material to be useful. While this is a personal statement on how the study of Confucius has affected my own outlook and practices, it is not a call for anyone to convert to Confucianism. Indeed, without a "church" of Confucianism or any official institution keeping it together, it is hard to know what such a conversion would entail. The project here has been simply to show how the serious study of another tradition does more than just fill your head with disinterested knowledge. If you take the worldview by which generations of people have lived seriously, it is bound to affect you in some way. In this final chapter, I will summarize the ways in which Confucius changed my mind. Those of you who study this or any other non-Western tradition may find your own minds changed in ways unique to you.

I will summarize my gains under three headings: the aspects of Confucianism that showed me new ways of seeing things; those that enabled me to peek under the hood of my native culture to see what its discourse obscures; and those that actually changed my practice in significant ways.

NEW IDEAS

Of all the new ideas that Confucianism opened for me, the deepest and most far-reaching in its implications was the view of the self as an interacting process instead of as a solid core. This ran counter to views I had always accepted in several ways. Having grown up with the biblical story of Genesis, in which God creates all creatures and endues them with essential characteristics, it came as news to me that the self is not only in constant flux but that this flux constitutes the self. Coming of age in a society that valued individual self-expression, one in which the constant message was that we need to find out who we really are and then align our lifestyle and actions to express our true natures, the Confucian idea that there is no solid core to be expressed seemed quite novel. I once took it for granted that there was a "me" in there and that the most important mission of my early life was to avoid hypocrisy by setting the direction of my journey so as to be true to myself. Confucianism suggested that *the journey is the self* and that "attaining the Way" is the most important moral task.

The notion that it is action, not being, that determines identity also took some getting used to, and in my teaching career I have found it to be difficult for my students as well. We assume that if a male human being has a child, then he *is* a father. He might be a bad or negligent father, but biology dictates that he is a father. Even when we have been raised by a stepfather who did everything perfectly so that our lives got off to a good start, we still wonder about our "real" father. This is in contrast with traditional Confucian ancestral practice in which the stepfather's memorial plaque sits upon the family altar and receives offerings and news, not that of the biological father who abandoned the family. The point is reinforced many times in Confucian literature, as when Mencius says he never heard of people rebelling against a king, only against a tyrant; or when a ghost is promoted to the status of a god because it begins accepting offerings and granting the petitions of supplicants not related by blood; or when the tradition affirms that one who does not develop toward greater humanity retreats into the status of an animal.

This is especially startling when it calls into question our idea of what it means to be human. Again, given our propensity to identify things by what they are, we assume that every baby born with human DNA is a human being and will never be anything else. Such an idea undergirds many things from our views on human rights to both the pro-life and pro-choice sides of the abortion debate. In the West, the question of whether you are human is black and white; either you are or you aren't. In contrast, the Confucian project of developing our humanity over the course of our lives means that this status is scalar; you can be more or less human at any moment. To think that you must first get on the path toward human thought and behavior and must follow it all your life, knowing that you will only approximate the human ideal more and more without ever completing it, is inconceivable within Western thought.

But this still misleads us since it portrays "the human" as a thing or a goal toward which we are moving. Combining this with the idea that the self is constituted by the journey, we arrive at a clearer picture. Our growth as humans does not mean that we become more human because we are continually approaching a static goal with fixed qualities. Humanity (*ren*) comes from being on the Way, aimed toward humanity, and moving ever forward. Being in motion makes us human as long as that motion is rightly oriented.

NEW VISTAS ON WESTERN CULTURE

The second way in which Confucius changed my mind was by leading me to recognize that much of our actual practices and behaviors do not align with our rhetoric of individualism and egalitarianism. In fact, Western cultural discourse, in emphasizing these features, prevents us from seeing the ways in which we often act like proper Confucians. These insights came primarily from observing how the porousness of our selves leads us to form bonds with others, and how these bonds come to expression in hierarchies and ritual conduct, sometimes in unexpected places. For example, once while watching a documentary on public television, I saw a reporter go to a venue where Insane Clown Posse was playing. This was a band whose members wore black shoes, pants, T-shirts, and clown makeup on their faces. Fans gathered in the parking lot before the show were all dressed this way as well. When the reporter asked one of them why he wore the clothes and makeup, he said with no trace of irony, "To show my individuality!"

This may be an extreme example, but when I look at society around me through the lens of Confucianism, I notice how infrequently I see anyone making a truly original fashion statement. In general, seeing the way someone dresses gives clues about the social group or ideology they identify with. In some segments of society, the social unit explicitly dictates dress: the military, schools that require uniforms, and professors on occasions that call for them to appear in academic regalia. These are cases in which, as Xunzi indicated, our group identity and status within that group literally stipulate who is entitled to some form of goods or services. In our multicultural and multilayered society, it seems that such choices as what we wear do not express individuality but the option we can sometimes exercise regarding which group we want to identify with.

Finally, contrary to our cultural rhetoric of free expression, I have found that many of the social situations that we navigate on a daily basis are governed by ritual propriety, though we may refer to it by other terms such as "etiquette" or "protocol." As noted before, I frequently point out to my students when teaching Confucianism that our class meetings run according to practices that we all absorbed during our socialization, and we assume a hierarchy in which we play different parts. As the professor, I am expected to plan the sessions and take a position in front of the class, and I have the floor most of the time. Students sit facing me, remain quiet, and raise their hands when they want to ask a question or make a comment. They also expect me to end the class on schedule, an expectation they will communicate by opening backpacks and shuffling papers noisily. This seems to be a recent development in classroom ritual. There is very little improvisation at play during the class period.

More broadly, the rhetoric of individualism has consistently prevented us from seeing the collective production of the conventions and morals that govern our social behavior. Westerners will still talk about the "social contract" without noticing that the idea of a "contract" would have to already exist for individuals to strike one to regulate their group life. Above, we saw an example of this blind spot in my student's uncomfortable question about eating babies, which betrayed his assumption that social practices come only from the agreement of free individuals. Under this assumption, it is easy to imagine that without a higher governing authority such as God to set the rules, individual caprice will be the only arbiter of right and wrong. Confucianism sees that society itself collectively produces its practices in much the same way that it produces language through experimentation. This process is invisible if we only see autonomous individuals making their own rules.

CHANGES TO MY OWN OUTLOOK
AND PRACTICES

In a few instances, my encounter with Confucianism has had an impact beyond merely showing me new possibilities that I might not have noticed had I stayed within a strictly Western cultural framework; it has convinced me to adopt some new practices. I will review two of the examples that I presented above. First, based on the Confucian inclination to emphasize dynamics over substance, or to classify things by what they do instead of what they are, I have changed my language in a few situations. I now prefer to say "I practice Buddhism" rather than "I am a Buddhist," and instead of saying "I am a vegetarian," I just say that I stopped eating meat. The result has been interesting. By expressing these as things I do rather than things I am, I avoid turning either of these choices into an identity. Statements of this kind feel less challenging and confrontational. This may be because putting matters in this way avoids the implication that I am part of a community that excludes my conversation partner. When they see that they are still part of my social horizon with no boundary between us, they are more likely to express curiosity about why I made those choices, and a dialogue sometimes takes off from there.

Second, accepting the Confucian assumption that many of our interactions take place in a ritualized manner and within hierarchical relations changed my teaching. Deciding to wear a coat and tie to class and assume a somewhat more formal manner than my students was the beginning. The results surprised me. The students responded positively to these changes because now our roles were clear and they knew how to proceed, whereas my prior attempts to be their equal and friend only made things unpredictable and inauthentic. To the objection I sometimes hear that this seems cold and rigid, I reply that in my experience, relationships, even when defined and embodied in this way, can still be very warm and inviting. I have said many times that Confucius convinced me to put on a tie, and this turned out to be wise counsel.

CONCLUSION

I hope that this final chapter has shown why Confucius is worthy of our serious study. If you decide to examine this tradition in a disciplined way, I do not know if it will affect you in exactly the same way that it affected me. You can only conduct the experiment and see what happens. I hope this book encourages you to try.

In broader terms, this book also shows why I took the study of other religious systems as my life's work and have enjoyed the pursuit for many decades. This study need not be confined to disinterested academic examination of facts and histories, and allowing yourself to be influenced by them does not have to take the form of conversion. If you dive in and ponder their teachings deeply, they can reveal new insights that would be hard to gain in any other way. At the same time, the process of uncovering the deeply ingrained cultural habits that block our way to grasping them helps us to better understand ourselves. In other words, looking at things from the Confucian perspective is like shining a light onto the landscape from a new angle. It is bound to reveal features that we would never have seen had we stayed within our own cultural horizon. To gain this understanding of self and others, we need to let go of two extreme views.

First, we must not assume that, based on our common humanity, other religions and cultures must be easy to understand. This causes us to project what we already believe onto others and to leap to the conclusion that all religions are basically identical. If this were true, it would mean we are not actually shining a light on things from a new angle after all, and nothing will be revealed that we did not already know.

Second, we must be wary of the assumption that "The Other" is so different from us that no real understanding across community boundaries is even possible. This leads us to give up on the task before it even begins. We gain no new insight into our life and world when we assume beforehand that the effort is futile.

In my experience, the truth lies in the middle. Interreligious and intercultural understanding is indeed possible, but it takes work, and that work is never complete. The longer you stay with the task by studying texts, learning languages, living for a time with another community, and many other ways, the closer you will come. In Confucian terms, first you "attain the Way" and then you apply yourself to treading that way for the long haul. To resort to the similarity with language one more time, a language learner may never attain true native proficiency, but if they keep up the effort over many years, they will constantly get better and be able to communicate more and more effectively. This book reflects where I am with Confucianism after thirty years of applying myself to understanding it. I hope that after more years of study, reflection, and interaction, I will have an even deeper understanding. Traversing the Way takes a lifetime.

Furthermore, I have found the task to be intergenerational. My study of Confucianism and other Asian traditions owes much to the seekers and scholars who attained the Way and walked it before me. In the sixteenth and seventeenth centuries, Jesuit missionaries mastered spoken and literary Chinese, and in concert with educated literati, translated the Confucian classics into Latin and circulated them in Europe. In the nineteenth century, diplomats and Protestant missionaries followed similar procedures to translate texts into European vernaculars and compiled commentaries and dictionaries. Throughout the twentieth century, missionaries, diplomats, and scholars continued the inquiry, always deepening our understanding of this tradition and correcting previous errors. Had it not been for these past efforts, this book would not have been possible. Perhaps it will inspire some of you to take up the calling and pursue intercultural and interreligious studies, leading in the future to new depths of understanding and transformation that I cannot presently imagine.

In 2011, Roger T. Ames wrote that the world was entering a transitional period in which, after two centuries of studied neglect, the Confucian tradition might come to the fore as a constructive resource for a rapidly interconnecting world. The West might begin to "appreciate" Confucianism, he said, not only in the sense of seeing it with increased affection but also in elevating its value.[1] If he is right, then this little book can serve as one step in that process. If in writing it and sending it out into the world I have cast a handful of new seeds, it is in the hope that the future harvest will be of benefit to individuals and salutary for the culture.

終

FOR FURTHER READING

Ames, Roger T., and David Hall. *Anticipating China: Thinking Through the Narratives of Chinese and Western Culture*. Albany: State University of New York Press, 1995.

This is a more academic book. Hall, a scholar of Western philosophy, and Ames, a specialist in Chinese thought, team up to present Confucianism in Western terms. The first section helpfully points out Western concepts that get in the way of understanding Confucianism before exploring key ideas within the tradition.

Chin, Annping, trans. *The Analects* (Lunyu). New York: Penguin, 2014.

There are many translations of the *Analects* available. I recommend this one because of the extensive and accessible annotations Professor Chin provides. These notes explain who the characters are, the historical situation of the different sections, the meanings of terms, and so on.

Fingarette, Herbert. *Confucius: The Secular as Sacred*. New York: Harper & Row, 1972.

Fingarette's book opened the study of Confucianism as a system of thought for Western scholars. It is short and easy to read, but it repays attention by helping readers understand the worldview and background that underlie the *Analects*.

Long out of print, it can be difficult to obtain, but it is worth the effort.

Puett, Michael, and Christine Gross-Loh. *The Path: What Chinese Philosophers Can Teach Us about the Good Life*. New York: Simon and Schuster, 2017.
This highly acclaimed book delves into ancient Confucian thought and offers more concrete suggestions on how to apply it to modern life.

NOTES

1. CONFUCIUS, MENCIUS, XUNZI, AND ME

1. "The Analects," trans. James Legge, Chinese Text Project, https://ctext.org/analects. All following quotes from *The Analects* are from this source.

2. RITUAL PROPRIETY, APPROPRIATENESS, AND THE CONFUCIAN SELF

1. Herbert Fingarette, *Confucius: The Secular as Sacred* (New York: Harper & Row, 1972), 9–11.
2. The way of relating ritual propriety to appropriateness given in these paragraphs owes much to Kwong-loi Shun, "*Ren* 仁 and *Li* 禮 in the *Analects*," in *Confucius and the* Analects: *New Essays*, ed. Bryan Van Norden (New York: Oxford University Press, 2002), 55–72, especially 62–70.
3. David L. Hall and Roger T. Ames, *Focusing the Familiar: A Translation and Philosophical Interpretation of the Zhongyong* (Honolulu: University of Hawai'i Press, 2001), 3–19; David L. Hall and Roger T. Ames, *Anticipating China: Thinking Through the Narratives of Chinese and Western Culture* (Albany: State University of New York Press, 1995), ch. 1.

4. The word *su* refers specifically to the Buddhist diet that eschews not only meat but also pungent herbs such as garlic and onions.
5. Charles Taylor, *A Secular Age* (Cambridge, MA: Belknap Press, 2007), 31ff.
6. Interestingly, the text of the *Analects* describes this as governing through *wuwei*, a term usually associated with Daoism. It is normally understood to mean taking no deliberative or calculating action and responding to the situation as it unfolds. This connection is not so surprising, however. Some scholars theorize that the foundational text of Daoism, the *Daodejing* of Laozi, originated as a political text giving advice to the king of a minor kingdom during the Warring States period.
7. "Da Xue" (The Great Learning), trans. James Legge, Chinese Text Project, https://ctext.org/liji/da-xue.

3. THE WAY (DAO)

1. Herbert Fingarette, *Confucius: The Secular as Sacred* (New York: Harper & Row, 1972), 18–36.
2. One of the difficulties in translating literary Chinese is that the same character, *xin*, can mean both "heart" and "mind." Often it seems that both are intended simultaneously.
3. Zhixu, "Pi xie ji: Collected Refutations of Heterodoxy by Ouyi Zhixu (1599–1655)," trans. Charles B. Jones, *Pacific World: Journal of the Institute of Buddhist Studies*, 3rd ser., no. 11 (2011): 369.

4. THE PRINCELY MAN, THE SAGE, SINCERITY, AND HUMANITY

1. Annping Chin, trans., *The Analects* (*Lunyu*) (New York: Penguin, 2014), 6.

2. Robert Eno, *The Confucian Creation of Heaven: Philosophy and the Defense of Ritual Mastery* (Albany: State University of New York Press, 1990), 64.

3. "Da Xue" (The Great Learning), trans. James Legge, Chinese Text Project, https://ctext.org/liji/da-xue.

4. "Zhong Yong" (Doctrine of the Mean), trans. James Legge, Chinese Text Project, https://ctext.org/liji/zhong-yong. All following quotations from the *Doctrine of Mean* are from this source.

5. David L. Hall and Roger T. Ames, *Focusing the Familiar: A Translation and Philosophical Interpretation of the Zhongyong* (Honolulu: University of Hawai'i Press, 2001), 11–15.

6. See the English text with Wing-tsit Chan's comments in Wing-tsit Chan, *A Source Book in Chinese Philosophy* (Princeton, NJ: Princeton University Press, 1963), 104.

7. See Charles B. Jones, "A Bundle of Joy: A Confucian Response," in *Ethics in World Religions: A Cross-Cultural Casebook*, ed. Regina W. Wolfe and Christine E. Gudorf (Maryknoll, NY: Orbis, 1999), 177–84.

8. Herbert Fingarette, *Confucius: The Secular as Sacred* (New York: Harper & Row, 1972), 51–52; romanization adapted to pinyin.

5. HUMAN NATURE

1. This is the same word that we rendered "appropriateness" when discussing Confucius.

2. See Wing-tsit Chan, *A Source Book in Chinese Philosophy* (Princeton, NJ: Princeton University Press, 1963), 54.

3. The air force equivalent of privates.

4. *Xunzi*, 20.1. Xunzi, like other ancient writers, is playing on the fact that "music" and "joy" were written with the same Chinese character, although using two different pronunciations.

6. PERSONAL CULTIVATION

1. Tu Weiming, *Confucian Thought: Selfhood as Creative Transformation* (Albany: State University of New York Press, 1985), 58.
2. See Wing-tsit Chan, *A Source Book in Chinese Philosophy* (Princeton, NJ: Princeton University Press, 1963), 86–87.
3. See Tu, *Confucian Thought*, 53.
4. Tu, *Confucian Thought*, 52.
5. Five of these are still extant. *The Book of Music* was lost very early in Confucian history.
6. Zhu Xi, *Learning to Be a Sage*, trans. Daniel K. Gardner (Berkeley: University of California Press, 1990), 129.

7. DISSENTERS

1. Mohism is named after its founder, Mo Di. In some sources, the name of this school is spelled "Moist," but many add a silent *h* to avoid confusion with the English word *moist*. *Daoism* was spelled *Taoism* in older English works. This reflects an out-of-date romanization system. *Daoism* accords with the standard pinyin system.
2. Wing-tsit Chan, *A Source Book in Chinese Philosophy* (Princeton, NJ: Princeton University Press, 1963), 253.
3. Chan, *Source Book*, 259.
4. Chan, *Source Book*, 259.
5. See Chan, *Source Book*, 253–54.
6. Brook Ziporyn, *Zhuangzi: The Essential Writings: With Selections from Traditional Commentaries* (Indianapolis: Hackett, 2009), p. 75.
7. Ziporyn, 85.

8. "Zhuangzi," trans. James Legge, Chinese Text Project, https:// ctext.org/zhuangzi.

9. Interestingly, in *Analects* 11.25, Confucius himself argues with a man who denies the usefulness of book learning for affairs of state.

8. HOW DID CONFUCIUS CHANGE MY MIND?

1. Roger T. Ames, *Confucian Role Ethics: A Vocabulary* (Honolulu: University of Hawai'i Press, 2011), 2.

WORKS CITED

Ames, Roger T. *Confucian Role Ethics: A Vocabulary*. Honolulu: University of Hawai'i Press, 2011.

Chan, Wing-tsit. *A Source Book in Chinese Philosophy*. Princeton: Princeton University Press, 1963.

Chin, Annping, trans. *The Analects* (Lunyu). New York: Penguin, 2014.

Chong, Kim-chong. *Zhuangzi's Critique of the Confucians: Blinded by the Human*. SUNY series in Chinese Philosophy and Culture. Albany: State University of New York Press, 2017.

Elman, Benjamin A. *A Cultural History of Civil Examinations in Late Imperial China*. Berkeley: University of California Press, 2000.

Eno, Robert. *The Confucian Creation of Heaven: Philosophy and the Defense of Ritual Mastery*. Albany: State University of New York Press, 1990.

Fingarette, Herbert. *Confucius: The Secular as Sacred*. New York: Harper & Row, 1972.

Hall, David L., and Roger T. Ames. *Anticipating China: Thinking Through the Narratives of Chinese and Western Culture*. Albany: State University of New York Press, 1995.

Hall, David L., and Roger T. Ames. *Focusing the Familiar: A Translation and Philosophical Interpretation of the* Zhongyong. Honolulu: University of Hawai'i Press, 2001.

Jones, Charles B. "A Bundle of Joy: A Confucian Response." In *Ethics in World Religions: A Cross-Cultural Casebook*, edited by Regina W. Wolfe and Christine E. Gudorf, 177–84. Maryknoll, NY: Orbis, 1999.

Miller, Alice. *For Your Own Good: Hidden Cruelty in Child-Rearing and the Roots of Violence*. 3rd ed. New York: Farrar, Straus and Giroux, 1990.

Taylor, Charles. *A Secular Age*. Cambridge, MA: Belknap Press, 2007.

Tu Weiming. *Confucian Thought: Selfhood as Creative Transformation*. Albany: State University of New York Press, 1985.

Van Norden, Bryan W., ed. *Confucius and the* Analects*: New Essays*. New York: Oxford University Press, 2002.

Zhixu. "Pi xie ji: Collected Refutations of Heterodoxy by Ouyi Zhixu (1599–1655)." Translated Charles B. Jones. *Pacific World: Journal of the Institute of Buddhist Studies*. 3rd series, no. 11 (2011): 351–407.

Zhu Xi. *Learning to Be a Sage*. Translated by Daniel K. Gardner. Berkeley: University of California Press, 1990.

Zhuangzi. *Chuang-tzu: The Inner Chapters*. Translated by A. C. Graham. Indianapolis: Hackett, 2001.

Ziporyn, Brook. *Zhuangzi: The Essential Writings: With Selections from Traditional Commentaries*. Indianapolis: Hackett, 2009.

INDEX

abortion, 75
    human rights and, 74–76, 139
    sex-selective, 74–75
action, 36
Ames, Roger T., 12, 21, 26, 68, 145
    appropriateness (*yi*), 19–25, 37
    meanings and translations of the
        term, 21–23
    ritual propriety and, 23–25, 37, 47,
        73, 78
    See also righteousness
authenticity, 22, 26, 32
    ritual propriety and, 31, 93, 94

balance. *See* equilibrium
being and identity, 28–29. *See also* self
Book of Odes (*Classic of Poetry*), 102,
    104, 106
boundaries, viii, 29–30, 51
Buddhism, 117
    Confucianism and, 134, 135
    enlightenment and, 45
    identifying as a Buddhist, 28, 142
    Jones and, 11, 28, 142
Bush, George H. W., 60

character, 102
Chinese classic texts, 104–5. *See also*
    Four Books and Five Classics
Christianity, 45, 52
Chu (state), 129–31
    king of, 129–31
Classic of Poetry. See *Book of Odes*
clothing, 31, 92, 93
Confucian *dao*, 40. *See also* Confucian Way
Confucian self
    nature of the, 100

as processive and porous, 25–30 (*see
    also* porous [Confucian] self)
    See also self
Confucian Way, 29, 40, 41, 54, 135
    human Way and, 47, 52 (*see also*
        human Way)
    the lessons, 54
    as a Way without a crossroads,
        40–43, 47, 54
    as a Way without a destination, 40,
        41, 44–47, 54
    See also Confucian *dao*; Way
Confucianism, 137–38
    new ideas from, 138–39
Confucius ("Master Kong"), 1–2
    background and life history, 4–7
    books about, 12, 76, 107–9
    bringing him into real life, 133–36
    death, 7
    on education, 100–101, 110, 132
    on humanity, 69–72, 76
    on learning, 1, 2, 33, 44, 46, 56
    legacy, 7–8
    names for, 5, 7
    princely man (*junzi*) and, 20, 21,
        56–57, 59–61, 65
    on ritual propriety. *See* ritual pro-
        priety
    on sages, 7, 44, 61, 63
Confucius: The Secular as Sacred (Finga-
    rette), 12, 76. *See also* Fingarette,
    Herbert
Cousin Elmo (character), 70–71, 73,
    74, 76
creativity, 68
Crouching Tiger, Hidden Dragon (film),
    39

dao, 39–40. *See also* Way
Daoism, 150n6
    terminology, 152n1
    See also Zhuangzi
Daoist critique, 133. See also *Zhuangzi*
Daxue. See *Great Learning*
disorder vs. harmony, 111, 112, 119
Doctrine of the Mean (by Zisi), 65–69,
    110, 111, 127
drives, instinctual, 83–84. *See also* human nature

education, 101–9, 113, 120, 121
    Confucius on, 100–101, 110, 132
    emotions and, 111, 112
    and the family, 103–4
    Hanfeizi on, 124, 125
    human nature and, 78, 80, 81, 85, 95
    humanistic, 6, 60, 95, 104, 109
    Mencius on, 80, 81, 88, 95, 110
    moral, 80, 88, 111, 118, 125
    poor/inappropriate, 85
    purposes, 100, 107
    qi and, 113–14
    questions regarding, 119
    self-cultivation and, 95, 100, 113
    Western culture and, 109, 119
    Zhu Xi on learning and, 107, 112–15,
        118, 119, 134–35
    See also learning; teachers
emotions, 111, 112
    arousal of, 111, 112, 116, 118
English language, 49–51
enlightened rulers, 59
enlightenment, 39, 45, 46. *See also* Way
Eno, Robert, 62–63
equilibrium, 47
    the mind at, 47, 110, 112, 116–18
    See also harmony
etiquette. *See* ritual propriety
evil. *See under* Mencius; Xunzi: on
    human nature

families, 74–75, 103–4
fear, 57
Fingarette, Herbert, 12, 17, 40, 41, 76
Four Books and Five Classics, 107–9
Four Sprouts (*si duan*), 83–89
    Mencius on, 83–86, 88, 89

Gaozi (Master Gao), 82–84

governance, 105, 124–25
    personal development and, 35
Great Learning (by Zengzi), 65, 67, 99,
    104, 107, 112–13
group identity, 140

Hall, David L., 12, 21, 26, 68
handshake, 17, 22, 51, 94
Hanfeizi, 122–25
harmony, 110, 111, 115, 118
    vs. disorder, 111, 112, 119
    See also equilibrium
Heaven, 128
    Confucius on, 3, 61
    cooperation of, 128, 129
    and Earth, 65–66
    Legalists and, 127, 128
    Mandate of Heaven, 3, 6
    Mozi on, 125–29
    Ouyi Zhixu on, 52
    sincerity and, 65–69
    and transformation, 65–66
    Xunzi on, 89, 97
    Yao and, 61, 63
    Zhou dynasty and, 3
Hui of Liang, King, 33–35
human nature, 79–81
    Confucius on, 79–80
    education and, 78, 80, 81, 85, 95
    human fulfillment and, 95–96
    inborn nature, 83, 84, 89–91
    meanings of the term, 10, 80–81
    philosophical question of, 79, 80
    See also under Mencius; Xunzi
human rights and abortion, 74–76, 139
human Way, 47–54
    dao as a, 98
humanism, Confucian, 47–48
humanistic education, 6, 60, 95, 104, 109
humanity (*ren*), 70–78
    Confucian vs. Western ideas/notions
        of, 74
    Confucius on, 69–72, 76
    DNA and, 74, 75
    etymology of the term, 72
    nature of, 69–78
    virtue of, 71–73
hypocrisy, 26

identity, 27–29, 138, 140, 142. *See also*
    self

inborn nature, 83, 84, 89–91. *See also* human nature
individualism, 48
    rhetoric and discourse of, 54, 140, 141
innate tendencies. *See* Four Sprouts
inner and the outer, the, 30–32
interactive self. *See* Confucian self
intuition vs. "mere book learning," 109

jing (classic), 104
Jixia Academy, 9, 10, 64, 80
junzi, 57–58, 60
    vs. *shi*, 58, 60, 64
    See also princely man

kings
    Mencius and, 27, 33–35, 139
    See also sage-kings

language, 48–51, 98
    ritual and, 17, 19, 22
    ritual propriety and, 23
language learning, 36, 98, 144
learning
    "book learning," 109, 119
    Confucius on, 1, 2, 33, 44, 46, 56
    language, 36, 98, 144
    memorization, 101, 102, 104, 106
    purposes, 107
    self-cultivation and, 98, 100, 103–5, 107
    terminology, 101
    Zhu Xi on, 107, 108, 119
    See also education; *Great Learning*
Legalists, 3, 123
    Heaven and, 127, 128
    Legalist challenge to Confucianism, 122–25, 133
li. See principle; ritual propriety

Mandate of Heaven, 3, 6
meaning, 62–63
memorization, 101, 102, 104, 106
Mencius, 8–10, 61, 134
    biography, 9
    on burial, 103
    Confucius and, 41, 42
    on education, 80, 81, 88, 95, 110
    on Four Sprouts, 83–86, 88, 89
    on human nature as wholly good, 10, 64, 80–89, 95, 111, 113, 116

on human vices and evil, 27, 34, 82, 85, 89–91
kings and, 27, 33–35, 139
vs. Mozi on universal caring, 103, 127
overview, 8–10
parables, 85–87
on ritual propriety, 21, 24, 83
on sages and sagehood, 61, 63–65, 85, 95
on sincerity, 67
on worthies, 82–83, 85, 86
Xunzi and, 9–11, 64–65, 67, 80–81, 89–91, 95, 111
Zhu Xi and, 113, 115, 116
Ming dynasty, 116, 117
Mohism/Moism, 103, 122, 152n1
    Confucianism and, 122, 123, 133
        Mohist alternative to Confucianism, 125–29
    ritual propriety and, 128, 129, 133
moral education, 80, 88, 111, 118, 125
moral mind, model of the, 110–19
morality, social, 48, 50, 51, 134
Mozi, 3, 103, 125–29
    on Heaven, 125–29
music, 21, 31, 68–69, 94

National Taiwan University, 36
neo-Confucianism, 134

Odes. See Book of Odes
one-child policy, 74–75
"order of operations" for training the self, 99–100
Other, the, ix, 144. *See also* self: and other
Ouyi Zhixu, 52
Ox Mountain, parable of, 86–87

peace, 35, 104, 105
personal cultivation. *See* self-cultivation
politics and politicians. *See* governance
porous (Confucian) self, 29, 34, 36, 37, 43, 50, 140
princely man (*junzi*), 56–60, 63
    Confucius and the, 20, 21, 56–57, 59–61, 65
    ideal of the, 62
    nature of the, 21, 56–57, 77, 97, 106
    ritual propriety and the, 20
    and the sage, 61–65

princely man (*junzi*) (*continued*)
  sincerity and the, 66, 67
  terminology and related terms, xii,
    55, 57–58, 62, 65, 67
  Xunzi on the, 64, 67
principle
  Zhu Xi on, 108, 113–16, 118
  See also ritual propriety
processive self, 27
professors, 32
propriety
  rules of, 15–16
  See also ritual propriety
protocol. *See* ritual propriety

Qi (state), 8, 27, 64, 80
qi (vital force), 113–16
Qing dynasty, 59

reading, Zhu Xi on, 107, 108, 113, 134, 135
religions, 135. *See also specific topics*
righteousness (*yi*), 23, 34, 83, 86. *See
    also* appropriateness
ritual
  language and, 17, 19, 22
  ritual propriety and, 15–19, 37
  Xunzi on, 11, 61–62, 94, 123, 128
ritual propriety (*li*), 99, 121, 122, 131,
    133
  appropriateness and, 23–25, 37, 47,
    73, 78
  authenticity and, 31, 93, 94
  clothing and, 92, 93
  Confucius on, 16, 19–21, 31, 42, 55,
    67, 100–101
  cultivation of, 37
  economic regulation and, 92
  emotions and violations of, 111
  family and, 75, 103
  heaven and, 6, 128, 129
  humanity and, 69–70, 73, 77–78
  and the inner self, 37
  Mencius and, 21, 24, 83
  Mohism and, 128, 129, 133
  nature of, 17, 23, 25, 129
  ritual and, 15–19, 37
  self-cultivation in, 95
  sincerity and, 67, 68
  terminology and related terms, 25,
    141
  and the Way, 42, 129

Xunzi and, 89–94
  Zhuangzi on, 129, 132
ru (class of men), 4, 5, 8, 58

sage-kings, 91, 95
sagehood, 64, 65, 86
  achieving, 62, 65, 115
  Mencius on, 63–65, 95
  self-cultivation and, 95, 97
sages
  ancient, 108, 113, 114, 123, 130, 134
  Confucius on, 7, 44, 61, 63
  meanings and notions of "sage"
    (*sheng*), 62–65, 67
  Mencius on, 61, 64, 65, 85
  nature of, 48, 63, 64, 77, 109, 115
  princely men and, 61–65
  ritual propriety and, 94
  sincerity and, 55, 67, 69, 73, 77
  terminology, 55, 64
  words of, 108, 113, 114, 130
  Xunzi on, 97
  See also "worthies"; specific sages
self, 26–30
  interactive, 37
  the journey is the, 138
  and other, ix, 33–37, 144 (*see also*
    inner and the outer)
  See also Confucian self
self-cultivation, 97–100, 107, 113
  education and, 95, 100, 113
  learning and, 98, 100, 103–5, 107
  studying and, 35–36, 97, 98,
    100–102
  Xunzi on, 62, 64, 94, 95, 97
Shang dynasty, 2–4
shi, 58, 60
  vs. *junzi*, 58, 60, 64
Shun, Emperor, 33–35, 58, 63
Sima Niu, 57
sincerity, 55, 65–67
  Heaven and, 65–69
  human nature and, 81
  meaning of, 66, 67, 69, 77
  overview and nature of, 66
  sages and, 55, 67, 69, 73, 77
  terminology and related terms, 67
  Zhu Xi and, 113
social contract, 50, 141
social conventions, 48, 50, 92, 141
social mores. *See* morality

Song dynasty, 4, 106–7, 111
Spring and Autumn period, 8
sprouts. *See* Four Sprouts
studying
    self-cultivation and, 35–36, 97, 98,
        100–102
    Zhu Xi on, 107, 115, 116, 118

Taylor, Charles, 29
teachers, 18, 61–62, 102
"to be," 28–29
Tu Weiming, 98, 104

utilitarianism, 126, 128, 129

Wang Yangming, 116–19
    Zhu Xi and, 116, 118, 119
Warring States period, 8, 122–24
Way, the
    attaining, 39, 45, 55, 74, 76, 88, 134–
        35, 144 (*see also* enlightenment)
    Confucianism and, 29, 40, 53, 55, 98,
        134, 144 (*see also* Confucian Way)
    and meanings of "way," 39–40
    Mencius and, 88
    natural impulses, training, and,
        90–91
    nature of, 39, 42, 43
    ritual propriety and, 42, 129
    rulers and, 63
    Zhuangzi and, 129, 132, 134
    See also *dao*
Western culture
    education and, 109, 119
    new vistas on, 140–41
wheelmaking and wheelwrights, 124,
    130, 132–33
"worthies" (*xian*), 82–83, 85, 86. *See also*
    sages
wuwei, 150n6

xue
    meanings and translations of the
        term, 101, 102
    See also studying

Xunzi
    on beauty, 11
    as Confucian, 94, 95
    Confucius and, 7
    on human nature, 64, 65, 89, 90,
        94, 95
        as wholly evil, 10, 80, 81, 88–95,
          111, 123
    Mencius and. *See* Mencius: Zunxi
        and
    on moral education, 81
    overview, 10–11
    on ritual, 11, 61–62, 94, 123, 128
    ritual propriety and, 89–94
    on sages and sagehood, 61–62, 65,
        91, 94, 95
    on self-cultivation, 62, 64, 94, 95, 97
    on sincerity, 67

Yao, Emperor, 58, 61, 63
yi
    meanings of the term, 22–23
    See also appropriateness; righteous-
        ness
You (philosopher), 15–16

Zengzi (Zeng Shen), 44–46, 97. See also
    Great Learning
Zhixu, Ouyi, 52
zhong, 47, 72
Zhou dynasty, 2–4
Zhou of Shang, King, 27
Zhu Xi
    on human nature, 113, 114
    on learning and education, 107,
        112–15, 118, 119, 134–35
    Mencius and, 113, 115–16
    on principles, 113–16, 118
    on *qi*, 113, 114
    on reading, 107, 108, 113, 134, 135
    Wang Yangming and, 116, 118, 119
Zhuang Zhou (Zhuangzi), 16, 130–34
    and the Way, 129, 132, 134
Zhuangzi (book), 129–30
Zuo Qiu Ming, 30

ABOUT THE AUTHOR

Charles B. Jones, a specialist in East Asian Buddhism, recently retired as ordinary professor in the School of Theology and Religious Studies at The Catholic University of America in Washington, DC, where he taught Asian religions, theories, methods in religious studies, and interreligious dialogue for almost thirty years. His works include *Pure Land: History, Tradition, and Practice* (Shambhala, 2021), *Buddhism in Taiwan: Religion and the State, 1660–1990* (1999), and *Chinese Pure Land Buddhism: Understanding a Tradition of Practice* (2019).